Mallorca and Menorca

120th anniversary

Berlitz®

- A ☛ in the text denotes a highly recommended sight
- A complete A–Z of practical information starts on p.103
- Extensive mapping on cover flaps

Berlitz Publishing Company, Inc.

Princeton   Mexico City   Dublin   Eschborn   Singapore

Text:	Martin Gostelow
Additional text:	Judith Edward, Brigitte Lee
Editors:	Hazel Clarke
Photography:	John Davison
Layout:	Media Content Marketing, Inc.
Cartography:	Visual Image

Found an error we should know about? Our editor would be happy to hear from you, and a postcard would do. Although we make every effort to ensure the accuracy of all the information in this book, changes do occur.

ISBN 2-8315-6312-7
Revised 1998 – First Printing March 1998

Printed in Switzerland by Weber SA, Bienne
019/803 REV

CONTENTS

MALLORCA AND MENORCA

THE ISLANDS AND THE PEOPLE

Millions of visitors every year flock to Mallorca and Menorca from the colder north, and many return year after year, attracted by the reliable sunshine and the warm, turquoise-blue sea; choice deals of flight, accommodation, and meals; cheerful service by friendly people who can understand your language; plenty to do—or nothing to do; sensuous indolence or an adventure playground. And all brilliantly organized to keep the cost down.

There's always been a lot more to the Balearics, as the island group is called, than just beaches and bars, of course. As activities augment or replace simple sunning, and the holiday season generally gets longer, the islands are attracting new admirers. Thousands of Europe's cyclists in rainbow gear take to the roads of Mallorca in March. April and May bring hikers to exclaim over the islands' wildflowers. Bird-spotters with binoculars and telephoto lenses compete to record rarities and migrants on their way north. By June, human migration in the opposite direction really starts to heat up. Many keep their boats here, anything from a dinghy to a millionaire's gin palace. This is a sailing paradise with safe harbours and marinas a short cruise from quiet coves.

Those who have never been here claim that the islands are loud and covered in concrete: Mallorca has sometimes had a bad press; Menorca has had hardly any press at all. Believe the negative noises and you'll miss out on two treasure islands that can't be duplicated anywhere. Loud? In summer, certainly, in the brasher places, but the sound comes from people having the good time they came for, in the company they like. If you want to avoid the hubbub, then you can. Concrete? It's there, yes, but is restricted to small areas. Climb to a hilltop and the resorts look like tiny white toytowns, mere pinpoints around the edge of undisturbed rural tranquillity.

Because previous generations moved inland to get out of range of marauding pirates, it means that today's islanders can live almost unmolested by the beach-bound majority of modern invaders. So, against the odds, much of the islands' traditional life and values have been preserved. However, the repeated waves of visitors bent on pleasure-seeking have inevitably had some effect on the local way of life. Farmland

---

Fact File

Geography: Mallorca and Menorca, in the western Mediterranean, lying about 180 km (110 miles) off the southeast coast of Spain, are the two largest of the Balearic Islands (the other principal islands are Ibiza and Formentera). Mallorca covers 3,640 square km (1,405 square miles) and Menorca 700 square km (270 square miles). Northwestern Mallorca is mountainous, with steep sea cliffs and few harbours. The southeast is hilly, the centre quite flat. Most of Menorca is gently rolling hills; the west is flatter.

Government: Spain is a democracy and a constitutional monarchy. The king is head of state. Since 1983, many of the powers of the central government in Madrid have been devolved to 17 autonomous regions, one of which is the Balearic Islands, with its regional capital at Palma de Mallorca.

Economy: Tourism is the major earner, though farming remains important (fruit, vegetables, grain, wine, and livestock), as does fishing. Industries include leather goods, salt by evapo,ration of seawater, artificial pearls, textiles, and ceramics.

Religion: Mainly Catholic (no longer the state religion), with small Protestant, Jewish, Islamic, and other minorities.

Languages: Spanish (Castilian) is used universally, especially in business and in dealings with Spain. Among themselves, local people use their own Catalan dialects, *Mallorquí* and *Menorquí*. English and German are also widely understood.

began to be left untended as people took jobs in the holiday industry or in constructing its facilities, although plenty of people still have "normal" occupations and are level headed on the subject of tourism. This is especially true on Menorca, where cold winter winds limit the season's length. That prudence should help to maintain a healthy economy, now that the number of visitors is stabilizing after years of unstoppable growth.

Islanders at work are a common sight. Here a woman peels garlic for cooking.

The islanders have a well-deserved reputation for hard work. On the building sites it often looks as if the labourers must be earning a bonus for every minute they save. Fishermen still put to sea in their double-ended boats, directly descended from Arab designs. Get off the tourist track and you'll find farmers cheerfully working lonely fields that look about as fertile as a main road. Their predecessors must have put the same sort of energy into shifting stone to build all the prehistoric villages, towers, and monuments found on the islands: it largely explains how a small population could have achieved so much.

Land sales for development as well as income from the influx of visitors have made the Balearics the most prosperous region of Spain. You'll notice how some of the money has been spent putting houses into good shape. The smallest village has its video rental "club," although there may be no other shops and nowhere to eat out. Parked cars threaten to choke every street. The ubiquitous noisy mopeds symbolize the new independence of today's teenagers, who used to have a strict upbringing.

The locals stay amazingly good-natured in the face of the foreign invasion, though their patience can get a bit frayed by the end of summer. It may be tested further as more visitors buy into the old towns and villages, instead of being content with the holiday centres. A quest for quality accommodation has resulted in more "country house" hotels in converted farms and mansions. Since these usually fill up almost immediately, further additions to the choice can be expected. Visitors are graduating, too, from sterile apartment blocks to houses and villas, to renting, buying, or time-sharing. They're demanding more trees and green space around them as well as much more imaginative architecture.

Traditional practices and the old way of life have not yet been wiped out by tourism.

Just in time (or rather late in the day), a powerful environmental conscience has found its voice, and campaigns have saved undeveloped islands and bays. The building of leisure facilities is now taxed by the regional government, and the proceeds used to buy land and keep it pristine. National parks and nature reserves have been established. So, the goose that laid the golden egg of tourism is to be a protected species.

A BRIEF HISTORY

By about 5000 B.C., there were people living in the Balearics. We can only guess where they came from; the coast of mainland Spain is nearest, but still quite a voyage. At first they lived in caves and rock shelters, and hunted the only large animal on the islands, a type of antelope, now extinct. They raised domestic livestock from about 3000 B.C., and later turned to growing crops as well. In a landscape strewn with rocks and boulders it was natural to build simple stone houses and to clear fields by piling the stones into heaps and walls.

By about 1200 B.C. construction had become more ambitious, as great towers called *talaiots* were being built; you can still find dozens in Mallorca and hundreds in Menorca. They may have been burial chambers, though experts disagree about their exact purpose. Useful as watchtowers, some became strong points in later defensive walls. They've given their name to a period and culture, the Talaiotic.

You can still see entire prehistoric villages of substantial houses, such as Capocorp Vell (see page 53) and Ses Paisses (see page 48) on Mallorca. On Menorca there's a feast of ancient architecture, such as ceremonial halls with roofs supported by rough columns, and *navetas*—burial chambers like upturned boats made out of stone. Most beautiful of all,

Dated at 900 B.C., the taula at Torralba d'En Salort is the most beautiful on Menorca.

and unique to Menorca, are the *taulas*, tall vertical stones, each supporting a horizontal slab in an elegant T-shape.

Another skill with stones was the islanders' deadly use of the sling, and it was this that brought them onto the world stage and into written history. Indeed, the name Balearic may come from the Greek *ballein*, "to throw." The Carthaginians absorbed the islands into their trading empire and founded the main ports, but they had learned to respect the slingers, and recruited thousands into their armies. In 146 B.C., at the end of the Punic Wars, the Romans defeated the Carthaginians but didn't immediately take over the Balearics. However, by 123 B.C. they had pacified most of Spain and sent out an invasion force. The Roman ships were protected by coverings of hide against the stones and lead shot of the slingers. Once in possession, the Romans named the islands—*Balearis Major*, which became Mallorca, and *Balearis Minor*, now known as Menorca.

The people continued to live in their villages around the *talaiots*, and the influence of the Romans on building seems to have been small. You can see that, at some sites, the conquerors merely reinforced the prehistoric walls, though they did found the towns of Palmaria (Palma) and Pollentia (near present-day Alcúdia). In the fifth century, as the Empire crumbled, tribes called barbarians by the Romans poured into Spain. Goths were followed by Vandals, in their turn pursued by Visigoths, who established themselves more permanently. The Vandals crossed to North Africa and there became a sea power to be reckoned with. They occupied the Balearics until defeated by a Byzantine expedition sent from Constantinople in 534.

The Tide of Islam

Ignited in the Arabian peninsula by the teachings of the Prophet Muhammad, the faith of Islam spread like wildfire,

HISTORICAL LANDMARKS

5000 B.C. First evidence of human habitation in the Balearics.

1200 B.C. Great stone towers called *talaiots* are first constructed.

123 B.C. Romans subdue the islands and name them.

A.D. 534 Vandal occupation of the Balearics is brought to an end by a Byzantine expedition from Constantinople.

711 Moorish invasion forces land near Gibraltar, and Spain eventually falls under Islamic rule.

848 Caliphs of Spain send out the navy to quell disturbances in the Balearics and to impose Islam.

1114 Christian crusaders overrun the island of Mallorca, but are forced to withdraw.

1229 The city of Palma falls to the Christian army of Aragón. Menorca agrees to pay tribute to Aragón.

1287 Alfonso III of Aragón invades Menorca, expelling the Moors and leaving the economy in ruins.

1349 Jaume III is killed in battle by Pedro IV of Aragón, bringing to an end the independent kingdom of Mallorca.

1492 Spain is united under Ferdinand and Isabella and the last Moorish enclave of Granada is taken.

1588 Spain's neglect of the Mediterranean leads to a succession of piratical assaults on the Balearics.

1702–1713 In the War of the Spanish Succession, the Balearics, with Britain and Austria, back the Habsburg claimant.

1708 Menorca taken by the British; ceded to Spain in 1802.

1808–1814 Spanish War of Independence; first constitution drafted.

1929 Spanish dictator Primo de Rivera falls from power.

1936–1939 Spanish Civil War. Menorca declares for the republic, while Mallorca is seized by Franco's Nationalist forces.

1975 King Juan Carlos I enthroned; transition to democracy. Renaissance in Balearic languages and culture.

1986 Spain joins the European Community (now EU).

with its armies reaching the Atlantic coast of Morocco by the year 683. Muslim converts in North Africa included the warlike, nomadic Berbers, or, as they became known, the Moors. They were determined to carry their new religion into Europe, and in 711 a predominantly Moorish army under the Arab general Tarik landed near the peninsula known from then on as the Rock of Tarik (*Gibel-Tarik* or Gibraltar). Within just seven years almost all of Spain was in Moorish hands.

The great Muslim world, from Baghdad to the Pyrenees, soon broke into fragments, and the Spanish part became an independent caliphate, with its capital at Córdoba. Under tolerant rulers the city rapidly became one of Europe's greatest centres of scholarship and the arts. At first the caliphs were content to accept tribute from the Balearics, without imposing Islam, but by 848 disturbances in the islands moved them to deploy their newly expanded navy to bring the region into line.

By the 11th century, the caliphate in its turn had splintered into a mosaic of fractious states—26 at one point. During the confusion, Muslim governors, including those on the Balearics, ruled as independent monarchs until waves of zealots came from Morocco to enforce greater unity in the face of Christian resurgence.

The Reconquest

The aim of the Crusades was not confined merely to regaining the Holy Land: even before Jerusalem was recovered in 1099, popes and preachers had been calling for the Muslims to be thrown out of Spain. There were countless setbacks, but Christian kings and warlords gradually succeeded in forging alliances that set them on the road to the Reconquest. In total, after the recovery of Jerusalem, it took a further four hundred years of sieges and battles, treaties, betrayals, and yet more battles before the Moors were finally overcome.

Muslim ports counted as targets for crusading, and a raid on Mallorca in 1114 overran most of the island before the attackers were forced to withdraw. On 10 September 1229, the Christians returned—this time for good—when a Catalan army led by King Jaume I of Aragón came ashore near the present-day resort of Santa Ponça. The defenders retreated inside the walls of Palma, but on the last day of 1229 the city fell and pockets of resistance throughout the island were soon mopped up. Jaume I was an enlightened ruler who made use of the talents of the Moors who had converted to Christianity, as well as of the island's large Jewish and Genoese trading communities; so Mallorca prospered.

The Moors on Menorca, on the other hand, had speedily agreed to pay an annual tribute to Aragón and were left in peace. That tranquillity lasted until 1287, when Alfonso III of Aragón, smarting over a series of humiliations at the hands of his nobles, found a pretext for invasion. The Moors were defeated and expelled or killed, thus leaving Menorca's economy devastated for decades.

Jaume I died after reigning in Aragón for 63 years, but he made the cardinal error of dividing between his sons the lands he had fought for so long to unite. At first this created a separate kingdom of Mallorca, under Jaume II, followed by Sanç and Jaume III. But family rivalry resulted in the overthrow of Jaume III by his cousin Pedro IV, who then grabbed the Balearics for Aragón. Attempting a comeback, Jaume was killed in battle near Llucmajor in 1349.

Progress towards a single, Christian Spain subsequently continued through conquests, alliances, and various strategic marriages until only Castile and Aragón remained. When the heirs of the two kingdoms, Ferdinand and Isabella, were married in 1469, the stage was set for the final act of the Reconquest. At last, a combined army was raised against the only Moorish enclave left on the Iberian peninsula, Granada, taking it in 1492. For the first time in history, Spain was united.

World Power

Even as one age ended, another was beginning. Before the final defeat of Granada was achieved, Isabella and Ferdinand had received Christopher Columbus. The captain from Genoa (at least three Mallorcan towns dispute that he was a Genoese and claim him as their own) believed he could reach the East Indies by sailing westwards. In the same year that Granada fell, Columbus crossed the Atlantic, landing in the Caribbean islands.

His feat marked the beginning of a century in which Spain exported its adventurers, traders, and priests, as well as its language, culture, and religion, to the New World, and created a vast empire. Ruthless *conquistadores* sent back incalculable riches of silver and gold. The century and a half after 1492 has often been called Spain's "Golden Age." Although in a literal sense it may have been that—in the arts it certainly was—the era carried the seeds of its own decline. Drained of manpower and ships by such adventurism as the dispatch of the ill-fated Armada against England in 1588, and plagued by corruption and incompe-

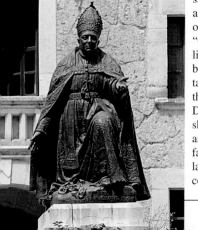

This statue of Bishop Campins at Lluc Monastery hasn't budged since the 13th century.

tence, Spain became ineffectual at defending her interests. The promising commerce of the Balearics was attacked by Muslim pirates based in North Africa as well as by the powerful Turkish fleet.

French and British Ties

The daughter of Ferdinand and Isabella had married the son and heir of the Holy Roman Emperor, Maximilian of Hapsburg. The Spanish crown duly passed to the Hapsburgs, and Spain remained in their hands until the feeble-minded Carlos II died in 1700, leaving no heir. France, whose interests perennially clashed with Spain's, seized the chance to install the young grandson of Louis XIV on the Spanish throne.

A rival Habsburg claimant was supported by Austria and Britain, who saw a powerful Spanish-French alliance as a major threat. In the War of the Spanish Succession (1702–1713), which followed, most of the old kingdom of Aragón, including the Balearics, backed the Habsburgs. Britain seized Gibraltar—in the name of the Habsburg claimant—and retained it even when the war was over. In 1708 Britain also took Menorca, to obtain the magnificent harbour of Mahón (Maó) for the Royal Navy; she hung on to it even when Bourbon forces captured Mallorca at the end of the war.

Menorca was to change hands between Britain, France, and Spain five more times in less than a hundred years. The British finally gave up the island amicably to Spain in the year 1802, under the terms of the Treaty of Amiens.

By 1805, Spain was once more aligned with France, and Spanish ships fought alongside the French against Nelson at Trafalgar. Napoleon came to distrust his Spanish ally and forcibly replaced the king of Spain with his own brother, Joseph Bonaparte. A French army marched in to subdue the country. The Spanish resisted and, aided by British troops

**The Castell de Bellver near Palma attests to the
long, troubled history of Mallorca.**

commanded by the Duke of Wellington, drove the French out. What British historians call the Peninsular War (1808–1814) is known in Spain as the War of Independence. It was at this time that Spain's first constitution was drafted.

Hopes of a constitutional monarchy were soon dashed, however, and the 19th century saw a succession of uprisings in restless regions, often in the name of parliamentary democracy. Practically all of Spain's possessions in the Americas broke away in the wake of the Napoleonic Wars, and the few that were left were lost at the end of the 19th century. The beginning of the 20th century was marked only by more crises, assassinations, and near anarchy. The colonial war in Morocco provided an almost welcome distraction, but a disastrous defeat there in 1921 led to a coup in which the general Primo de Rivera became dictator. He was able to enforce public order and initiate public works, but could only, in effect, screw down the lid on the pressure cooker. He fell in 1929, and when the elections of 1931 revealed massive anti-royalist feeling in Spain's cities, the king followed him into exile.

The Republic and Civil War

The new republic was born in an orgy of strikes, church-burnings, and uprisings of the right and left. Elections gave first the left, then the right, a majority. Elections in February 1936 gave the left-wing Popular Front the majority of seats in the *Cortes*, but in the country at large new extremes of violence were taking the place of argument.

In July 1936, most of the army, led by General Francisco Franco—with the support of the monarchists, conservatives, the clergy, and the right-wing Falange — rose against the Madrid government. Ranged on the government's side were the Republicans, including liberals, socialists, Communists, and anarchists. The ensuing Civil War was fought with a great deal of savagery and bitterness. Support for both sides came from outside Spain. Many people, frequently unaware of the particularly Spanish origins of the struggle, saw it as a contest between democracy and dictatorship, or, from the other side, between order and Red chaos. Fascist Italy and Nazi Germany backed Franco's Nationalists, while the Soviet Union supported the government (although less towards the end). The war lasted three years; the dead were uncounted, but estimates range up to one million.

At the start, Menorca declared for the republic, and stayed with it to the bitter end. Mallorca's garrison seized it for the Nationalists, as Franco's forces were known. Early in the war, the Republicans used their one battleship to support an invasion of Mallorca, but it ended in failure. A decisive factor was the presence at Palma of Italian air squadrons, used to bomb republican Barcelona.

New Horizons

Exhausted, Spain was able to remain on the sidelines during World War II and began to recover under the continuing tough law-and-order regime of Franco. There had been a foretaste of foreign tourism in the 1920s, though of a rather exclusive variety. So the tourist trade that began in the 1950s and exploded into an annual rush by millions of sun-seekers was a new phenomenon, with a profound impact on the economy and the people. One effect was a rash of building on the coastline, at first with scant regard for tradition or aesthetics. Less visible, though perhaps more significant, was the influx of foreign influences into Franco's once hermetically sealed Spain.

Franco named as his successor the grandson of Alfonso XIII, who was enthroned as King Juan Carlos I when the dictator died in 1975. There were dire predictions of a short reign, of violence, even of a renewal of civil war. In complete contrast to most of his forebears, the king proved to have a genius for reconciliation and common sense. To the dismay of Franco diehards, he managed brilliantly the transition to democracy, then stood back to allow it full rein. After many years of repression, a great deal of autonomy was granted to the Spanish regions, including the Balearics, and their languages and cultures enjoyed a renaissance.

More a part of Europe than ever before, Spain joined the European Community (now European Union) in 1986, giving a further boost to her booming economy. The new dawn brought a realization that unrestricted growth of mass tourism had damaging consequences. There developed a new emphasis on quality and, especially in the Balearics, on safeguarding the environment. That, after all, was largely why people had wanted to visit in the first place.

WHERE TO GO

Whether you're in Palma, a coastal resort, or an inland village, you can reach any point on Mallorca in half a day, and Menorca is even more concentrated. Tour companies offer excursions by road or in combinations with a boat trip, to see the mountain and coastal scenery of the northwest, the beaches, the spectacular caves near the east coast, and various purpose-built attractions. At these sights you'll inevitably be part of a crowd, especially in high season.

Hiring a car (see page 106) lets you go where you like—some of the least-known places are the most delightful —or you could use the buses or rent a bicycle. In the height

Fuel types for cars/trucks:
unleaded (*sin plomo*)
regular (*gasolina*)
premium (*super*)
diesel (*gasóleo*)

of summer you should travel in the cool of the early morning or make use of the long evenings.

Below the city walls, Palma's Parc de la Mar is the ideal place to take in the sun.

We start our journey in and around Palma, then make the tour of Mallorca in a clockwise direction, taking in all the highlights and plenty of diversions before finishing up in the centre. You can join in at any stage, and head back to where you're staying when you have had enough. Menorca rates its own section (see page 58).

We don't try to mention every village or every beach: it would take a lifetime of holidays to see them. You'll need several visits just to cover the selection here. For more ideas see also our list of beach highlights on pages 51 and 71.

PALMA DE MALLORCA

Almost two-thirds of the permanent population of Mallorca live in Palma, and a glance at the map shows how the island's road system radiates from the city.

The romantic way to arrive is from the sea at dawn or sunset. If you can't contrive to sail in on a sleek car ferry or a yacht, at least try to take a boat trip in the bay so that you see Palma from its best angle. From the bay you can see, dominating the centre of the city, the great Gothic cathedral, with the ancient Almudaina Palace below it. To the east is Platja de Palma, a long line of sandy beaches that stretch through Ca'n Pastilla to S'Arenal; to the west stretches the elegant promenade of modern Palma, where luxury hotels look out over a forest of masts in the yacht harbour. Crowning the wooded slopes above it are the white towers of Bellver Castle.

On shore, a tour begins in the old part of the city (*Centre Historic* on direction signs). On the waterfront, fishermen lay out their nets. Palm trees drop dates on the bayside boulevard, something of a racetrack for local drivers. Parts of the old city walls facing the sea still stand; the rest were levelled long ago into a girdle of avenues.

MALLORCA HIGHLIGHTS

(See also Beach Highlights on pages 51 and 71.)

Aquacity: *Autovia Palma–El Arenal 15 km (9 miles), tel. 49 07 02.* Europe's biggest water amusement park; open daily, May 10am-5pm, June-September 10am-6pm. (See page 88)

Cathedral (La Seu) and Museum: *Palma, tel. 72 31 30.* Beautiful Gothic building; Gaudí altar canopy and ancient manuscripts; open November-March 10am-3pm, April-October 10am-6pm, Saturday until 2:30pm, closed Sunday and fiestas. (See page 25)

Coves del Drac: *Porto Cristo, tel. 82 07 53.* Huge caverns and underground lake; visits daily November-March 10:45am, 12pm, 2pm and 3:30pm, April-October daily on the hour 10am-12pm and 2pm-5pm; entrance includes tour and concert. (See page 49-50)

Ferrocarril de Sóller: *Plaza d'España, Palma, tel. 75 20 51.* Spectacular mountain railway from Palma to Sóller; open-top trams to the Port of Sóller. The 10:40 train has a view stop. (See page 39)

La Granja: *Esporles 14 km (9 miles), tel. 61 00 32.* Living museum of rural Mallorcan life; open daily 10am-7pm (until 6pm in winter), Fiesta Mallorquín every Wednesday and Friday 3:30pm-5pm, including folk dancing and sampling of local food. (See page 35)

Marineland: *Costa d'En Blanes, Calvia, tel. 67 51 25.* Aquatic fun for all the family; open daily, September-March 9:30am-5pm, April-August 9:30am-6:45pm, closed 20 November-25 December; dolphin and seal shows from 11am. (See page 88)

Poble Espanyol: *Palma, tel. 73 70 75.* Spanish architectural treasures and craft workshops in cleverly designed replica village; open daily, winter 10am-6pm, summer 9am-8pm. (See page 29)

S'Albufera: *Muro, tel. 89 21 59.* Nature reserve and important water-marsh area; open daily 9:30am-6pm for cars, otherwise entrance on foot; phone for guided visits on Wednesdays. (See page 46)

Sa Cartuja: *Valldemossa, tel. 61 21 06.* Old Carthusian monastery visited by Chopin and George Sand; traditional Mallorcan dancing, Palace of King Sanç Monday and Thursday at 10:30am; piano concerts every other day 10:30am-6:50pm. (See page 36)

The old city is full of pleasant surprises (though avoid unpleasant ones by not carrying valuables that can be snatched in summer crowds). Walking is the way to see them best—distances are quite small and many streets are reserved for pedestrians. If you'd like to treat yourself to a tour in one of the horsedrawn open carriages, try to choose a Sunday when other traffic is light.

Below the walls, the **Parc de la Mar** is too unshaded and bare for local strollers, despite its lake and a tile panel by Catalan artist Joan Miró. They prefer the gardens of **S'Hort del Rei**, next to the Almudaina Palace, though it's a matter of debate as to whether Alexander Calder's mobile *Nancy* belongs here. Most of all, they like **Es Born**, the elongated plaza that runs inland, for their early evening promenade.

Get a feel for the history of Palma with a stroll through the centuries-old back streets.

Following the line of the moat of the Arab city, it was the site of jousting tournaments. Now, it's lined with park benches and cafés where businessmen meet over coffee and tourists rest their feet. At the top of Es Born, **Avinguda del Rei Jaume III** imitates the architectural style of a century ago, although it's actually much more recent. Here, expensive shops reflect the sophistication of a city made rich by the tourist trade.

The **Palau Almudaina** was once the palace of the Moorish rulers. After the

Reconquest it was remodelled for use by the kings of Mallorca. Part of it is open to visitors, and a short tour takes in the superb stone-vaulted 13th-century throne room, divided into two storeys in the 16th century—you'll see that the window was cut off in the process. In the heavily restored royal offices, which are used by the present king and queen, traces of early paintwork survive on ceilings and frescoed walls. In the palace courtyard, dominated by the west front of the cathedral, the royal chapel of Santa Ana has a rare Romanesque doorway from the 14th century.

The massive Gothic **cathedral** (*La Seu*) was begun in 1230, after the Christians recaptured the island from the Moors, and stands on the site of the former main mosque. Building was slow and sporadic, affected by wars and finance, and it was 1601 before the great work was completed.

Finding Your Way

With the resurgence of the islands' own dialects, places and streets previously named in Castilian Spanish on signs and maps are now usually given in local forms. Both may be used interchangeably, causing visitors some confusion.

Ca'n, which appears in so many place names, originally meant "house of," and *Son*, "estate or farm." *Bini*, derived from Arabic, signified "the sons of" (i.e., family). *Cala* means "cove."

English	Mallorquí/Castilian	English	Mallorquí/Castilian
Avenue	Avinguda/Avenida	Market	Mercat/Mercado
Road	Camí/Camino	Palace	Palau/Palacio
Street	Carrer/Calle	Passage	Passaig/Pasaje
Castle	Castell/Castillo	Boulevard	Passeig/Paseo
Centre	Centre/Centro	Square	Plaça/Plaza
Cave	Cova/Cueva	Beach	Platja/Playa
Church	Església/Iglesia	Town	Poble/Pueblo

Closely packed buttresses facing seaward create an extraordinary effect of power—and beauty, too, when they blaze like gold in the setting sun. They had defensive value, as there was always the threat of bombardment from the bay. If you walk round to that side you'll see the remarkable *Mirador* entrance.

The north door of the cathedral, near the 13th-century bell tower, is open only in the early morning and early evening. At other times, you have to go in through the nearby **Cathedral Museum**, which is a treasure-store of old manuscripts, relics of saints, and portable altars. A colossal carved-stone Renaissance doorway leads on to the oval New Chapter House.

In the spacious cathedral itself, there are just 14 unusually slim columns supporting a soaring roof. The windows are fewer and smaller than is usual in north European churches. When the sun shines, however, the stained-glass windows—some pictorial, most gaudy and geometric—let in brilliant rainbows of sunlight. The Crown of Thorns canopy over the high altar was added by Catalan architect Antoni Gaudí at the beginning of the 20th century.

The **Palau Episcopal**, on a quiet square at the east end of the cathedral, is the home of the Diocesan Museum, with a diverse collection accumulated by various archbishops. The houses in the narrow streets behind the cathedral are so tall that they seem to meet overhead. Some are baronial **mansions** from the 15th and 16th centuries, with dark walls and great wooden doors. They may look forbidding, but try to get a glimpse through the heavy metal grilles into some of the courtyards. The **Casa Oleo** in Carrer Almudaina retains its Gothic architecture; even older is the Arab **Almudaina Arch** which crosses the same street. Many courtyards were remodelled in the 18th century, including **Casa Oleza** (in Carrer Morey), with its wide-arched, cool patios and its balconies and stately staircases.

In the nearby Carrer de la Portella a palatial mansion has been restored as the **Museu de Mallorca**. The labelling is in Spanish only, but the relics of the Muslim period and fine 13th- to 15th-century paintings and carvings, originally from Palma's churches, make the museum worth a visit. The top floor houses exhibitions by present-day Mallorcan artists. Old photographs show some of the Arab gateways that were destroyed when the city walls were razed in 1902. The **Arab Baths** (*Banys Arabs*),

The Arab baths are worth a visit, if only to see the lovely gardens that surround them.

behind the museum in Carrer Serra, are miraculously still standing after one thousand years. The horseshoe arches of the domed bathhouse are supported by capitals in various styles—no doubt taken from earlier buildings. As in the Roman manner, the steam room had underfloor heating, and the vaulted room next door would have been the cooling-off area.

The **Basílica de Sant Frances** (Basílica of St. Francis), on the Plaça Sant Frances, is one of Palma's treasures. In front of the building stands a statue of Junípero Serra—18th-century founder of the first missions in California. Inside the church lies the sarcophagus of the 13th-century sage and teacher Ramón Llull. He and Serra are two of Mallorca's greatest sons and heroes—they have both been beatified, and sainthood seems sure to follow. An effigy of Llull is perched high up in a chapel behind the altar, with beautifully carved 14th-century stone niches below. Be sure to walk through to the enchanting cloisters: their slender double columns and stone tracery are from the same time.

You may have noticed another statue of Llull near the Almudaina Palace. Just to the west are two Palma landmarks standing side by side. The turreted **Sa Llotja** was built in the 15th century by local architect Guillermo Sagrera (the seafront promenade is named after him). Once the city merchants' exchange (now used to house exhibitions), it is one of Spain's finest secular Gothic buildings. Slim columns twist through its light and airy interior to the vaulted roof. Next to Sa Llotja, a cannon and an anchor surround the 17th-century **Consolat del Mar**, the former maritime law court—now the seat of the Balearic Islands' autonomous government.

Statue of the famous missionary Junípero Serra, in front of the Convento de Sant Francesc, Palma.

The **Plaça Cort** is the site of the fine wooden-eaved 17th-century Ajuntament (or Town Hall) and from there it's a short way by smart shopping streets to the **Plaça Major**, the former market-place. This has been restored and paved with glossy marble, though unfortunately the face-lift has not yet brought the area back to respectability after dark. Today's market is under cover at the **Mercat** in Plaça Olivar.

On Saturday mornings the crowds flock to the **Baratillo**, or Flea Market (even the signs on city buses call it by its English name). Here you're sure to find everything from fans to fossils, and bargains include Mallorca's artificial pearls and lace—offered at "liquidation" prices by the sellers.

In the area of the Poligon de Llevante quarter east of the old city is the **Museu Krekovic**, housing strikingly gaudy images from Inca and Spanish history—products of the overheated imagination of a Yugoslav-born artist.

When the evening promenade disperses, the streets of the old city are usually quiet, dark, and practically deserted. There is more action if you head west to **Es Jonquet**, once the fishermen's quarter, now full of bars, cafés, and clubs clustering under the old windmills which used to grind the city's flour. On the seafront, the **Auditorium** furnishes a panoply of entertainment from opera to heavy metal. Farther on, five-star hotels stand between the sea and the suburb of **El Terreno**, where Avinguda Joan Miró and the Plaça Gomila are lined with cafés, discos, and topless bars. Once the centre of Palma nightlife, the area is struggling to keep from being third-rate.

A few hundred metres inland from Es Jonquet, the **Poble Espanyol** is a brilliantly designed walled town of replicas (some scaled down) of Spanish architectural treasures from places including Toledo, Seville, and Córdoba, as well as the Alhambra of Granada. The place is a multi-level maze, fitting and flowing so cleverly that there are no dead ends—even if you climb up the stairs. The buildings are not mere façades, but house shops, craft studios, bars, and cafés. The number of people going through have given it all the patina of age. Across the street, the same sort of inspiration has created a Convention Centre in the form of a Roman forum and theatre.

You won't have been able to miss the fine sight of **Bellver Castle** (*Castell de Bellver*), on its hilltop above the modern Palma among pine trees and parkland. A magnificent piece of military architecture, it has commanded the sea and land approaches to the city since it was built in the 14th century by order of King Jaume II. The view from the circular battlements is stunning, and you'll see how the sloping roof funnelled rainwater into the castle's cisterns. Inside, there's a small, well-laid-out museum of the archaeology of the area. When you're hungry, head for the hillside village of Genova and its choice of restaurants.

THE BAY OF PALMA

Two sweeps of white sand made Palma's magnificent bay a summer magnet, and the resorts that are spread out along them gave Mallorca a name for cheap and cheerful holidays.

Bellver Castle has been an imposing landmark on the hilltop since the 14th century.

That picture has always been oversimplified: there's a lot of choice, including the most luxurious and expensive.

East: Platja de Palma

The southeastern shore of the bay runs through former fishing villages to the beach resort and yacht harbour of Ca'n Pastilla, almost at the end of the airport runway. Then come Las Maravillas and S'Arenal, a 7-km (4-mile) strip of hotels, fast food restaurants, loud bars and discos, British pubs and German beerhalls. Restaurants range from the "English-Owned—No Oil Used" type to several rather good Mallorcan ones. The narrow streets of the seafront area can be a riot of fun and noise—day and night. And you'll have to pick your way across the beach through another sea of tightly packed bodies.

West Side of the Bay

To the west of Palma, **Cala Major** ("great cove") has been a holiday centre since long before the package tour boom. The British royal family has a summer home here and uses it as a base for sailing. At Sant Agustí and Illetes you can swim off the rocks or along the small sandy beaches—some man-made—and stay at hotels with an old-established air, where you'll wake to the sound of waves. Alternation of rock and sand continues past more-exclusive Bendinat up to Portals Nous, where apartment blocks cluster on the slopes. The glamorous-looking marina of Puerto Punta Portals is not natural but ambitiously carved out of the cliffs.

Sandy beaches start again at Costa d'En Blanes, home of **Marineland** with its dolphin displays, and of Palma Nova, which blends gradually into big, brash **Magalluf**. Here the ranks of hotels and apartment blocks mark another burst of mass tourism facilities. The wide and sandy beach, sloping safely into the sea, can hardly be seen in summer for browning bodies. Bars a block long, discos built like airport terminals, restaurants offering menus in eight languages from Finnish to French, waterslides, go-karts — you name it, Magalluf has it. Except for tranquillity. For that, you have around 95 percent of the rest of the island to choose from.

West of Magalluf, the road leads towards the golf course. To the south, the once-quiet cove of Cala Vinjes has been practically covered with concrete in a wild orgy of overbuilding. Continue on through pine woods to the Casino de Mallorca and by narrow winding lanes to the pretty coves and beaches of **Portals Vells**. Here, in the cliffs, you'll find huge rock-cut caverns dating from Roman times or earlier, and enlarged over the centuries. Boats make the short excursion from the pier on Magalluf beach. Not far south of Portals Vells, you can hike to a very quiet cove, the Cala Figuera (don't confuse it with others of the same name). Farther on the road is blocked: the end of the peninsula is a military zone.

THE WESTERN TIP

King Juan Carlos likes to drive his guests round a circuit to the west of Palma, showing them the stunning scenery of coast and mountains. You might like to take a leaf out of the royal tour book.

The main road bypasses the resorts of the Bay of Palma and meets up with the sea once again at **Santa Ponça**, where a cross on a headland marks the landing place of King Jaume I and his Catalan army in 1229, which began the campaign to recapture Mallorca from the Moors. Dramatic reliefs on the base of the memorial depict the event. Sandy beaches and the sheltered bay now attract another sort of invasion, although Santa Ponça is a decibel or two less noisy than the loudest resorts. It boasts one of the widest ranges of sports, and keeps going out of season, too, with an older clientele. So does neighbouring **Peguera**, with similar facilities.

The pleasantly tree-shaded beaches of **Cala Fornells** are still picturesque, although hotels and clusters of villas press closely round. Camp de Mar, with its big, plain hotels on the next inlet, has more sand but less charm. A scenic but twisting little road leads to **Port d'Andratx**, a broad, wonderfully sheltered bay that is home to more yachts than fishing boats these days. The old harbour area on the south side keeps its traditional appearance, though a closer look reveals a string of restaurants, and the slopes facing it across the water are encrusted with villas and apartments. You can swim off the rocks; lack of a sandy beach has kept the big hotels away, which is just fine with most visitors. Just a short drive, brisk walk, or morning jog takes you 3 km (2 miles) to the **Cap de**

Escape Magalluf and its crowds with a visit to the pretty, quiet coves of Portals Vells.

Sa Mola, the most southwesterly point on the island, with its superb views of sheer cliffs and shining sea.

The main road inland leads to the port's "twin" town of **Andraitx**, made up of brown stone houses and a maze of little one-way streets that puts foreign motorists to the test. Many Mallorcan towns (Pollença and Sóller are other examples) are built like this one, several miles from the sea that brought them trade and fish. The main reason for the inland site was the marauding pirates, though in most of the smaller harbours there was little room for building anyway. Topped by a fortress-like 13th-century church, Andraitx seems to ignore the rest of the world, and most traffic simply passes by on the edge of town.

From Andraitx, a dead-end road leads to the coast at **San Telm** (Sant Elm)—a former fishing village which doesn't try too hard to be a resort. The view offshore from its mostly stony little beaches is dominated by the island of **Sa Dragonera**, subject of a long legal battle between would-be developers and conservationists. It seems likely that the lizards which gave the island its name will be left in peace.

Head inland and enjoy authentic charms of Andraitx and its 13th-century church.

You can head back to Palma from Andraitx by means of country roads, passing through farmland and orchards and the prosperous towns of Capdella and Calvia. If you don't mind more hairpin bends than an Alpine pass, go the longer, adventurous way round through Galilea and Puig-punyent, stopping to take in the views.

NORTHWEST: COAST AND MOUNTAINS

The most dramatic stretch of Mallorca's coastline faces the Spanish mainland. The mountains sweep down to the sea so steeply here that there are few points of access and only one harbour and port of any size. The road winds along clifftops, providing a series of vertigo-inducing viewpoints, frequently giving up any attempt to stay close to the water and mean-dering into the mountains instead. North of Andraitx, it reaches the first of a succession of **miradors**, high places with a commanding prospect of the coast. Some of them are still crowned with an ancient watchtower, from which look-outs anxiously scanned the sea for pirate ships and signalled warnings to the next point along the chain. If possible, you should make the trip early in the morning, or you'll be part of a procession from one parking spot to the next.

At **Estellencs**, an ancient town amid terraces and orange groves, you can walk or drive down a track to a little fishing cove. Back on the main road, take in one of the best views, from the snail-shaped tower of **Ses Animes** ("the spirits"). The hillsides around the town of **Banyalbufar** have been tamed since Moorish times into some of the finest terraces on the island. A small lane twists down to a rocky cove and a small beach, while another reaches the sea at Es Canonge. Facilities in the area are few, but despite this—or because of it—the few hotels that exist have their quiet adherents, and villas are going up.

North of Banyalbufar, the road turns its back on the coast for a while. Just off the road, in the direction of Esporles, you'll find **La Granja**, a combination of a stately home, a traditional farmhouse, a craft centre, and a living museum of rural Mallorcan life. You may see a potter or blacksmith at work in the shade of the massive outbuildings and cellars. You can sample local wines, sweet and fortified, or orange and lemon cordials. Here, too, are children's play areas, gardens to stroll through, geese and ducks, sheep with their bells tinkling donkey rides, and sometimes country dancing. The fountains and ponds are fed by springs first channelled by the Moors. Inside the house, everything appears to be estate-made, and it probably was: the furniture is folksy, and walls are painted to look as if they have been papered. Friendly staff, some in traditional dress, demonstrate the weaving of cloth, carpets, and ribbons, lacemaking, and embroidery. The estate itself belonged to Cistercian monks before it came to the Fortuny family, which still owns it.

The town of **Valldemossa** was transformed by the short visit, over a century and a half ago, of French writer George Sand and her lover, Frédéric Chopin. Their few weeks here in the winter of 1838–1839 seem to have been fairly miserable: Chopin was unwell, the weather was wet and cold and bad for his chest, and George Sand despised the local people, describing them in her book *A Winter in Majorca* as "barbarians, thieves and monkeys." The locals can't have thought too highly of her—a scandalous woman who not only smoked and wore trousers, but had left her husband to live with another man.

 Now, busloads of visitors come almost daily to see the couple's lodgings in the former Carthusian monastery **Sa Cartuja**. The monks had been expelled in 1835, and some of their cells were sold as holiday apartments. The word "cells" perhaps gives a false idea; in fact, each is a suite of three rooms with a private garden. The two cells that the lovers rented are now a museum dedicated to them, with original manuscripts, Chopin's death mask, and his piano. You'll see,

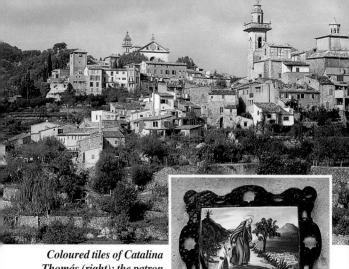

Coloured tiles of Catalina Thomás (right); the patron saint of Valldemossa (above) decorates many doorways.

too, the massive church, the monks' pharmacy with its collection of 18th-century jars, their library, and the guests' dining room. (The monks ate alone in their cells, served through hatches) The adjacent "Palace of King Sanç" has only a very tenuous link with the 14th-century Mallorcan king.

The daytime tourist invasion seems to swamp Valldemossa, but by evening time the town is able to sit back and breathe again, and the cool early mornings can be idyllic. At least as significant to Mallorcans as their Chopin connection is the fact that, in 1531, Valldemossa was the birthplace of their own saint, Catalina Thomàs. You can see statues of her in churches all over the island, and coloured tiles bearing her image decorate nearly all the doorways in Valldemossa.

There couldn't be a greater contrast to George Sand's negative impressions of Mallorca than the lifelong love affair that the Austrian Archduke Ludwig Salvator (or Luis Salvator) had with the Balearics and their people. In 1870 he bought the estate of **Son Marroig** (just outside Deià). The house, which is open to visitors, is filled with his collections. In the gardens, take in the bird's-eye view from the cliff-edge temple built out of Italian marble. **Na Foradada**, the rocky headland jutting into the sea hundreds of feet below, is pierced by a remarkable 18 metre- (60-foot-) wide natural window. If you feel energetic, take the half-hour's walk down to the sea and the landing stage where the archduke and his guests used to come ashore. A swim off the rocks will refresh you for the hard march uphill.

Nowadays they would be called "ex-pats," these foreigners who came to Mallorca and stayed. **Deià**, a pretty hilltop town of honey-coloured stone, has attracted plenty, ever since Robert Graves, the poet and author of *I, Claudius*, came to live here with Laura Riding in 1929, followed by a strange coterie of admirers. In later life he became the Grand Old Man of Deià, fierce in his defence of it against touristic exploitation. It comes as a shock to learn that in his early days here he tried to set himself up as a property developer, intending to build a hotel. One or two mansions in the vicinity have quite recently been turned into country-house hotels, which tend to be full from the time they open in spring. Summer brings film producers and rock stars who take houses in the town. Daytime tourists see little of this: Deià presents mainly closed doors to them as they walk up to the top of the hill. There, in the cemetery near the church, a simple cement slab bears the inscription: *Robert Graves, Poeta, 1895–1985*.

It's a long and twisting drive down to Deià's tiny fishing cove, where ladder-like ramps come out of the boathouses set into the cliffs. A snack bar and a beach café open in summer, but the rocky shore can get choked with seaweed. If you take a picnic, watch out: the place is alive with hungry cats.

At Sóller and its seaside twin **Port de Sóller**, the cliffs and mountains at last relent. The biggest bay on the northwest coast makes a fine harbour, but is so enclosed that both the water and the beach can be dirty. Sheltered slopes a few miles inland are covered in groves of lemon, orange, almond, and olive trees, with the island's highest mountain, **Puig Major** (1,445 metres/4,740 feet high), as a rugged

Rail fans—and anybody else — can take a trip on the tram to Port de Sóller.

backdrop. Sóller is a busy, prosperous town that claims like many others that it was the birthplace of Columbus. Trams travel every half-hour through lemon groves to Port de Sóller, continuing along the waterfront there. Sóller and Palma are linked by a narrow-gauge **electric railway**. Five times a day (six on Sundays), polished wooden trains make the hour-long journey in each direction through orchards and spectacular mountain scenery, stopping at Son Sardina and Bunyola. The 10:40 A.M. "special" from Palma takes in an extra scenic halt above Sóller.

If Sóller and especially its port look French—there is a reason. In past centuries, they were cut off by the mountains from the rest of the island, so that trade with France became a mainstay. Growing holiday business has brought new hotels and apartments around the bay, mercifully without quite spoiling the look of the waterfront. Fishermen still bring in their catches to the harbour, and right opposite is a line of restaurants that suit most budgets.

Two pretty villages near Sóller have enticed foreigners to buy houses and tourists to come and look. **Fornalutx** is a jewel of warm stone that looks as if it intends to win a prize as "best-kept place in Mallorca." Some of its cobbled streets climb in steep steps up the hillside. Similarly set among orange trees and wild flowers, **Biniaraix** is only a short stroll away down narrow lanes.

The authorities felt that the road from Palma to Sóller, with its hairpin bends and the 496-metre (1,627-foot) pass, the Coll de Sóller, was impeding development. In spite of vigorous protests from those who wanted to preserve the area the way it was, plans were approved for a road tunnel under the mountains, and digging began in 1990.

On the southern slope, right opposite the tunnel entrance, the seigneurial mansion and gardens of **Alfabia** were once the country estate of the Moorish Vizier of Palma, though they have been much altered since. These days, the cisterns, fountains, and irrigation channels are rather run down, but the flowing water and shaded walks, turkeys feeding under fig trees,

---

Fire

Forest fires (*incendio*) are a menace on Mallorca, particularly in the mountainous north where the only way to fight them may be by aerial bombardment. On Menorca, as well, undergrowth may be tinder-dry. So be careful where you throw matches and cigarette ends. Any campfires must be doused with water and covered with earth before you move on. In some areas signs indicate a complete ban on fires.

Footpath near Escorca. It's easy to escape the crowds and enjoy the island's wild scenery.

birds singing among exotic plants, and places to sit down and have a cool drink nevertheless exert a gentle attraction. The house is like a forgotten palace, full of neglected treasures. Don't miss the huge wooden 14th-century chair in the print room, called by one expert "the most important antique in Mallorca." The gatehouse ceiling, though it has been restored and often repainted, is basically a 13th-century Moorish creation.

The hilly country to the east of here, reached via Bunyola, is a favourite with walkers based at the little village of **Orient** or coming for a day's trip from the coast. A massive mountain crag 822 metres (2,700 feet) high is crowned by the **Castell d'Alaró**, a ruined fortress dating from the Moorish era. You can make the long walk from Orient, or drive most of the way to the summit up narrow and tortuous lanes, starting a little north of Alaró. The higher they climb, the rougher the tracks get, so you'll need an agile vehicle, not too big, low-slung, or heavily laden. The final ascent has to be on foot up rocky paths—wear sturdy walking shoes. The

The winding roads on the Cap de Formentor are certainly not for the faint-hearted.

gates and walls of the castle still guard the clifftop, and the views are as thrilling as any on Mallorca.

Forced away from the sea by the steep terrain, the main road north from Sóller climbs over the high pass of Coll de Puig Major and past the dams and reservoirs of Cuber and **Gorg Blau**. By the roadside near the second of these stands a battered old stone column, rescued, so a sign proclaims, from the flooding of the valley. Near the dam, a little road sets off to the coast. Its name, **Sa Calobra** ("the snake"), gives a hint of the 13 km (8 miles) of hairpin bends which have now become a tourist attraction in themselves, starting with one loop so exaggerated that the road passes under itself in a knot. If you are driving, early morning is the time to avoid the traffic. The light is better, too, on the strangely fluted and sharp edges of eroded limestone, interspersed with ancient olive trees. As a reward at the bottom of the winding road, Cala de Sa Calobra has a restaurant, bars, and a pebbly beach. The main objective is one of the wonders of Mallorca, the deep gorges of the **Torrent de Pareis** ("the twins"). Tunnels, enlarged from natural crevices in the rock, burrow through to the riverbed where the gorge widens into a natural theatre (concerts are given on some summer evenings). The beautiful little beach at the point where the gorge meets the sea can be crowded, so if you want more solitude, and if the river is as dry as usual, walk back along it between cliffs hundreds of feet high. The four-hour hike down the gorge from the main road near Escorca is demanding. You should go adequately prepared, and preferably with a companion.

At the **Monasteri de Lluc** foreign visitors are frequently outnumbered for once by local people, for this is Mallorca's favourite place of pilgrimage. It was founded in the 13th century, but the massive buildings you see today date from the 17th and 18th centuries. The islanders come to see and pray to a statue of the Madonna and Child, **La Moreneta** (or "little brown one"), so called because of the dark colour of its stone surface. There are many legends about its origins and adventurous history. One says it was found here and taken to a nearby church. During the night the statue disappeared, only to be rediscovered where it had originally been found. As this happened twice more, a chapel was built over the site and later the monastery grew up. You'll find the statue itself behind the high altar. Set into the two crowns are diamonds, emeralds, and pearls which have been donated over the years by Mallorcans. If you can attend mass in the church, you may hear the famous Lluc boys' choir, Es Blavets ("the blue ones"), named after the colour of their cassocks.

NORTHEAST: CAPES AND BAYS

Plenty of arrivals at Palma's airport make a beeline for the northeast coast and its two great sandy bays.

Port de Pollença is the kind of place that gives Mallorca a good name—with a perfectly sheltered, gently sloping sandy beach, a spectrum of hotels, *hostals*, apartments, and villas, a selection of restaurants, and some not-too-rowdy nightlife.

These days, there are luxury craft in the harbour and flotillas of windsurfers in the bay.

Many excursion boats sail round the spectacular cliffs of **Cap de Formentor**, the narrow headland jutting out 13 km (8 miles) on the north side of the bay.

Signs:
entrada - entrance
salida - exit

By land, try the beautifully engineered road along the cape, pausing where everyone else does (it's still worth doing) at the giddy viewpoint not far from Port de Pollença. Most boats and cars stop at the pine-shaded beach (Platja de Formentor or Cala Pi), a favourite spot for a picnic, swimming, and taking a look at the luxurious Hotel Formentor and its gardens.

Situated a few miles from the sea, to make it harder for corsairs to attack, **Pollença** was founded in 1230 after the defeat of the Moors. The name comes from the old Roman capital of Mallorca, Pollentia, sited some miles away near Alcúdia. Until 1802 the town belonged to the Order of the Knights of St. John, and many handsome stone buildings in the centre date from their time.

Whether Pollença's bridge labelled *Pont Roman* is really Roman is questionable, but the locals say so, and the tourists all photograph it. Most of the visitors go to the parish church in the town centre to climb up the shallow steps of the **Calvari,** lined with 365 cypress trees, to the tiny church at the top. (There's also a road up, passing the 14 Stations of the Cross.)

From the top of the Calvari steps, you can look across to the much higher **Ermita del Puig de María**. Find the little turning south of town, and you can drive most of the way up, negotiating the alarming hairpin bends and praying not to meet anything coming down. Eventually the road gives out, and the last ten minutes of the rewarding ascent to the fortified monastery at the summit are made on foot.

One of the best walks on Mallorca can be made only on a Saturday. Pollença is again the starting point, but this time head north, taking the narrow road towards **Ternelles**. Cars usually can go just a short distance before reaching a checkpoint where they have to turn back. However, on Saturdays during spring and autumn the landowners open their "frontier" to allow walkers only to go through (even cyclists are prohibited). The route follows the gorge of the Torrent de Ternelles at first, then turns off to head for the ruined **Castell del Rei**, built by the Moors on a soaring crag 500 metres (1,640 feet) above the sea. Another rough track leads down to the shore at Cala Castell, and the whole walk is about 13 km (8 miles).

Another pleasant walk is over the hills from Port de Pollença to **Cala Sant Vicenç,** twin sandy coves with brilliant blue water, excellent for swimming and snorkelling. Less dramatic than the Formentor peninsula is **Cap d'Es Pinar,** separating the Bay of Pollença from the still bigger Bay of Alcúdia. You can't go to the end—it's a military zone—but several little rocky coves and beaches make the Cap worth exploring. Astride the neck of land between the two bays stands the ancient walled town of **Alcúdia.**

The breathtaking Cap de Formentor can be enjoyed from boat or from car.

Too close to the sea for safety from raids, it must have been dependent on its impressive fortifications, rebuilt in the 16th century. The sturdy church of Sant Jaume in fact forms the southern bastion in the walls.

Beyond the road that circles the town you can see the low ruins remaining from Roman Pollentia. They're not impressive as such sites go, but some fine relics excavated here are now displayed in the little **museum**, a beautifully restored building opposite Sant Jaume church. Just off the road leading from Alcúdia to its port is the **Roman theatre**, hewn out of solid rock in the first century B.C. The slope is quite gentle, so it wasn't sufficient just to cut steps for the seats: grooves had to be made between the rows, or the spectators' knees would have been under their chins. The site was later used as a cemetery.

Port d'Alcúdia has evolved from a small fishing harbour into an all-purpose port for commercial, naval, and pleasure craft (there's a big yacht marina) and a summer resort. Restaurants and discos have multiplied. Hotels and apartment blocks have spread ever farther round the bay to form an almost unbroken ribbon of buildings 10 km (6 miles) long.

A small pier off Port d'Alcúdia serves as a vantage point for beautiful views.

Behind the coast, Llac Gran ("big lake") and the precious wetlands of **S'Albufera** are a haven for birdlife. Drainage schemes in the 19th century ran into such problems that the British company responsible for a network of canals, paths, and bridges—still to be seen today—went bust

thereafter. You can now walk or cycle among the 800 hectares (2,000 acres) that have been designated a *Parc Natural* (nature reserve), looking for some of the 200 species of birds that have been spotted here.

EAST COAST: COVES AND CAVES

Tiny harbours, some no more than a half-hidden cleft in the cliffs, alternate with the larger bays along Mallorca's eastern shore. A dwindling few are almost undiscovered, and others carry on fishing while welcoming an annual invasion of visitors. Some sheltered marina developments hold rows of millionaires' sleek white status symbols. Here and there, great clusters of villas turn from ghost town to boom town as soon as summer arrives.

Cala Ratjada is just about as far as you can get from Palma without having to take to the water. But the water is what most people are here for, whether it's the fishermen or the holiday-makers who vastly outnumber them in this lively resort. The tourist information office can arrange a visit to the **Juan March Sculpture Garden**, showing works by Rodin, Henry Moore, Barbara Hepworth, and many modern Spanish masters.

Sand beaches are close by at Cala Guya and Cala Molto, and there's a fine view of the coast from the lighthouse on Cap Capdepera. If it's clear, you'll be able to see Menorca. On the 271-metre (889-foot) peak of Jaumell, the next headland to the north, there was a semaphore station for signalling between the islands, in the days before radios and telephones (and when the air was clearer). The cape takes its name from **Capdepera**, where you can walk round the battlements of the 14th-century castle on the hill above the town.

The country town of **Artà,** 8 km (5 miles) inland, seems far removed from tourism. No hotels, but prosperity brought by the holiday business has nevertheless rubbed off. Here, as elsewhere, money has been spent on upkeep: the place has probably never looked better. Steps lead up by a Way of the Cross to the fortified church of Sant Salvador, where you get a fine view of the town, hills, and coast.

A sign pointing down a side road in the southern outskirts of Artà says simply "Talaiot," but it leads to one of Mallorca's most important megalithic settlements, **Ses Paisses**. Hidden among trees, the foundations of its rough buildings are ringed by walls of huge stones, with one massive gateway still intact. The site, dated to 1200–800 B.C., was probably occupied throughout Roman times.

Some distance away on the coast, Artà has given its name to the limestone caves called **Coves d'Artà**. The entrance, a great arch in the overhanging cliffs, is at the top of a long flight of steps. More steps (this is not a place for the immobile) take you down into vast chambers full of stalactites and stalagmites resembling groves of trees or piles of broccoli. One slender pillar has climbed to 22 metres (72 feet) and has only a little way to go to reach the ceiling—but don't hold your breath; it will take 5,000 years. Coloured lights and Bach's organ music point up the name given to the lowest level, "The Inferno." Jules Verne is said to have been inspired by a visit here to write *Journey to the Centre of the Earth*.

The road to Canyamel, a sandy bay shaded by pines, passes by the restored 14th-century **Torre de Canyamel** and Mallorca's most easterly golf course. The south-facing Costa del Pins has an exclusive air, unlike Cala Millor, a long stretch of sand and rocks backed by a solid wall of hotels and apartments. Adjoining Cala Bona is somewhat quieter. Inland, Son Servera has a Friday market—an authentic slice of Mallorcan life.

How about a safari as a change from the beach? The **Reserva Africana** has a reasonable selection of wildlife—

The unusual fortified church of Sant Salvador in Artà offers panoramic views.

antelopes, elephants, rhino, and ostriches. Vehicles pass slowly through the 40-hectare (100-acre) park, and although there are no dangerous predators, you are requested to stay in your car and close the windows.

S'Illot, Cala Moreia, and Cala Morlanda are developing into standard big white clusters of villas and hotels, by a white sand beach, but neighbouring **Porto Cristo** is something special. It's a popular holiday place, but fishermen still set out from the old port, which is concealed and sheltered from the sea by an S-bend inlet (unfortunately too narrow for the water and beach to be flushed clean). In 1936, after the start of the Civil War, the Republicans landed a large force here in an unsuccessful attempt to take Mallorca from the Nationalists.

Two groups of caves in the vicinity of Porto Cristo make a cool change from the beach—and attract a procession of tour buses. The highly commercial **Coves del Drac** (Caves of the

Stalagmites and stalactites greet visitors to the cavernous Coves d'Artà.

Dragon), to the south of the port, contain almost 2 km (more than a mile) of huge chambers and spectacular formations, as well as the un-questionable highlight—a 177-metre- (581-foot-) long underground lake named after Edouard-Alfred Martel, the French speleologist who explored the caves in 1896. Another feature is the *son et lumière* show that most caves go in for. A little way inland, the smaller **Coves dels Hams** are named after the fish-hook shapes of some of the stalac-tites. There's a succession of chambers with beautiful for-mations, a much smaller lake than the one at Coves del Drac, and, again, the coloured-light-and-music show. For an inland excursion, Manacor and Petra (see page 56) are not far away and worth exploring.

The perfect harbour setting of **Porto Colom** has been little changed by the tourism boom. Boathouses line the waterfront below the prettily painted houses of the fishermen. Commer-cial activity and the very narrow outlet to the sea mean that the water and the beaches inside the harbour can get dirty, but there are sea beaches close by. For an inland excursion head to Fe-lanitx and on to the hilltop castle of Santueri (see page 57).

Cala d'Or came early to the resort business, and it has now evolved into a huge complex, with all the facilities and watersports you could ask for, though the small beaches be-

MALLORCA: BEACH HIGHLIGHTS

Mallorca's big resorts have sandy beaches with easy access and good facilities. Below are some more coves and beaches—clockwise from Palma. (For Menorca's beaches, see page 71.)

Cala Portals Vells: Three small coves, with fine sand, good road access, and a number of facilities, including bars, restaurants, snack bars, and pedalboat hire. Cala El Mago is a nudist beach.

Cala de Valldemossa: A delightful rocky cove and fishing village at the end of a precipitous road. Several restaurants open in summer, one in winter. Swimming from rocks.

Cala Deià: A beautiful rocky cove, with short walk to the beach. Restaurants and transparent water. Crowded in high summer.

Cala Tuent: A well-kept secret off Sa Calobra road—breathtaking scenery, pebbly beach, crystal-clear water, and good snorkelling.

Cala Sant Vicenç: Three small coves with fine sand and transparent water, but dangerous strong undertow when rough. Good road access and facilities, including bars, restaurants, and pedalboats.

Platja de Formentor: Beautiful bay with rocky inlets, fine sand, and pebbles. Easy road access and ferry from Port de Pollença. Excellent facilities: snack bars, pedalos, waterskiing, windsurfing.

Badia d'Alcúdia: The longest beach on the island is excellent for children, with 17 km (10½ miles) of fine sand. On the south side of the bay, Son Serra Marina and Colònia de San Pedro are quieter.

Platja de Sa Coma: Fine white sand, near protected natural area of Punta de n'Amer. Easy road access. Beach facilities include bars, restaurants, pedalboats, windsurfing, waterskiing, sailing.

Porto Colom: Two beaches: sheltered Sa Punta inside the port, Cala Marcal outside. Busy July and August, deserted other times. Easy road access and good facilities: bars, restaurant, pedalboats.

Porto Petro: Cala Mondragò is an excellent small sandy beach in a beautiful rocky cove. Snack bar, restaurant, and pedalboats.

Colònia de Sant Jordi: Es Trenc is a long, wide beach with white sand, transparent water, and dunes. Access via a drivable track near Ses Salines. Several bars and other beach facilities.

come overloaded in summer and you can get lost in the net-work of roads. The yachts and cruisers tied up at the marina have an expensive air. In contrast, nearby **Porto Petro** still looks like a traditional fishing village, though it, too, is not immune from the summertime tourist invasion.

Cala Mondragó is practically undeveloped, and may stay that way by order of the regional government, which has be-come alarmed by the spectre of unchecked building along the coast. One of the gems that first attracted visitors to this part, **Cala Figuera** is still delightful, with neat houses and unpretentious boats lining its Y-shaped inlet.

THE SOUTH

Few visitors knew anything of Mallorca's deep south until recently. The long sandy beach of **Es Trenc**, for example,

Stroll among the yachts and rub shoulders with the jet set at the ultra-modern Cala d'Or.

was left to the islanders to enjoy, though a few pioneering nudists did establish themselves near Ses Covetes. The situation is changing a little. Roads from both Campos and Santanyi have been improved and a few signposts erected; even the nudists are now official. But it seems that major development won't be permitted.

Ses Salines takes its name from the local salt flats and ponds, where many bird-watchers gather in the spring to see the migrants on the way north from Africa. **Botanicactus** is a 15-hectare (37-acre) botanic garden specializing in cacti.

Colònia de Sant Jordi was a rather half-hearted attempt at a resort, but the nearby harbour of **Campos** serves as the starting point for trips to **Cabrera**, an island usually visible 17 km (11 miles) to the south, which got its name from the herds of goats that grazed on it from ancient times. Visits are limited to parties of bird-watchers or zoologists and to excursion groups, who get an hour and a half ashore for a walk, a swim, and a picnic. Excursion boats sometimes make the trip to Cova Blava, Cabrera's "Blue Grotto," which can be reached only from the sea.

Some 5 km (3 miles) inland from Cala Pi is found **Capocorp Vell**, the most remarkable of Mallorca's prehistoric settlements, situated 6 km (4 miles) from Cap Blanc on the most direct road towards Llucmajor. The site itself is clearly indicated, and there is a small café. The modest admission charge covers the loan of a brief guide and plan but, disappointingly for such an impressive site, there is nothing in the way of interpretation. From as early as 1200 B.C., massive stones were being cut and hauled into place to build a village. The remains you see today are more than 200 metres (650 feet) long, but traces of other buildings cover a much wider area. The five *talaiots* (three round towers, two square) may have been added later. Climb to the top of one for a good view of the site and

beyond. In this impressive place you can walk through doorways leading into complete rooms, and agile explorers can
wriggle several yards down the winding passage under one of
the towers (take a light). It leads to what was once, presumably, a burial chamber for tribal chiefs. Remarkably, its olive-
wood roof is still partially intact.

THE CENTRE

The local name, **Es Pla** ("the plain"), doesn't sound sopromis-
ing. Certainly not enticing enough to slow down fun-seekers
as they rush across the middle of Mallorca to get to their
favourite piece of coast and avoid the heat. But make an early
start, or choose a cooler day, and rewards are waiting. For the
growing numbers of spring and autumn visitors who come to
cycle, walk, and spot birds and wild flowers, the plain is ideal.

The main towns, along the busiest roadways, are not Mallorca's most attractive ones. But take any back road and
you'll discover little villages untouched by tourism, and see
farmers still using horses for ploughing. Stretching from the
highlands of the northwest to the hills of the southeast, the
plain is not as flat as its name implies. Peaks suddenly stick
up, crowned with an ancient monastery or castle ramparts;
and the views over orchards and fields are wonderful.

On the busy road northeast from Palma, the palatial former convent at **Santa María del Camí** now houses shops
selling the locally made wines and leather goods, and a folk
and archaeological museum. Turn
off the main road for the attractive
part of **Binissalem**, centre of Mallorca's wine production.

Signs:
Ilegada - **arrival**
salida - **departure**

The face of **Inca**, centre of the
leather industry (with several factory outlets), is marred by
ugly apartment blocks. However, it's worth exploring the

narrow streets and visiting the monastery cloisters of Sant Frances before picking one of the old wine-cellar restaurants for some traditional Mallorcan food. Inca's Thursday market sprawls through the streets; tour buses come in flotillas, although the goods are much the same as in other markets on the island.

Rich farmland surrounds **Sa Pobla**, and some of the battalions of windmills still pump water from wells first dug by the Moors a thousand years ago.

The pretty country town of **Muro** has a fine example of a Mallorcan arcaded

Windmills are still used in rural Mallorca to operate complex irrigation systems.

church, and an elegant town house built around a courtyard and garden has been restored as the home of the ethnology section of the **Museu de Mallorca**. Though short on labelling, the displays of traditional tools, old carriages, and pottery are worth seeing, and the house itself is the star exhibit.

Sineu, practically at the centre of the island, is the site King Jaume II chose to build a palace; it survives, now much altered, as a convent. The railway, which today runs only from Palma to Inca, used to come to Sineu and on to Manacor and Artà, and the track is still there, albeit overgrown or buried for most of the way.

Petra, a little inland town, is fairly typical of the plain, with warm brown stone houses fronting directly onto its quiet streets. Junípero Serra, a Franciscan friar with probably the best claim to be called the founder of California, was born here in 1713. When an expedition was sent from Mexico by order of King Carlos III in 1768, his task was to set up the chain of missions along the Pacific coast that eventually grew into today's cities of San Diego, Los Angeles, San José, San Francisco, and others. Visitors can look around **Casa Serra**, the house where he was born. It has a low second storey (note the little four-poster bed upstairs) as well as a pocket-sized garden. In the **Museu Serra** are displayed tributes from today's Californians and paintings and photographs of the missions the friar founded. They are also shown in tile panels along Carrer California next to the church.

In Mallorca, you don't get pearls from oysters. They're made in **Manacor**, the largest town after Palma but less than one-tenth the size. The place has an industrial look about it, and most of the traffic gratefully takes the road that bypasses the centre. Interesting old defensive towers and some fine stonework are not enough to compensate for the trouble of reaching them, except perhaps on a quiet Sunday morning. The pearl-makers have enterprisingly set up shop on the highway, and you can take a tour of their factories too. At the busiest times you'll be part of a production line yourself— as thousands of visitors troop daily through the factory. In the century-old process, glass beads are coated with a lustrous glaze made of powdered fish-scales and resin. After this is baked on, it's hard to tell the result from a real pearl.

At the town of **Felanitx**, the honey-coloured church dates in part from the 13th century. Its lovely west front, at the top of a huge and elegant flight of steps, is from the 17th century. In the street alongside is a stone tablet commemorating a tragedy. During an Easter procession in 1844, the collapse of a wall killed no fewer than 414 people. Some unusually good pottery is made in the town, which also used to be renowned for its cartographers—who Mallorcans claim furnished Columbus with maps (if and when they're not claiming Columbus himself).

Felanitx is the starting point for a bracing trip to **Castell de Santueri**, a ruined hilltop castle that was fortified by every ruler from Roman times to the 17th century. Take the exhilarating walk round the ramparts—there's nothing between you and a dizzying precipice. The views of the coast are superb, and on a rare clear day you'll see Menorca and Ibiza too.

On the next hill to the north—and unless you're a serious walker you'll have to go back through Felanitx to reach it— the **Puig de Sant Salvador** is the site of a hermitage and one of Mallorca's most important places of pilgrimage. In the church, look behind the altar at the Gothic statue of the Virgin Mary, backed by an alabaster panel of blond angels. In the gatehouse is a 5-metre- (17-foot-) long Gothic panel of the Last Supper, in wood and plaster.

Suddenly rearing up out of the flat lands south of Algaida, the 542-metre- (1,778-foot-) high **Puig de Randa** is crowned by a monastery founded in the 13th century by the Mallorcan sage Ramón Llull. There are two more monasteries tucked into the shelter of cliffs on the way up. They're all reached by the same narrow, twisting road, and it's worth stopping at each as you make the ascent, if only to see the panorama of the plain unfold. **Llucmajor**, the attractive town just south of Randa, was the site of the battle of 1349 in which Jaume III was defeated and killed by the forces of his cousin, Pedro IV of Aragón. It's a sad date for many islanders, for it brought to an end, after only 120 years, the story of the independent kingdom of Mallorca.

MENORCA

Menorca is one-fifth the area of its neighbour, with a tenth the population and the same small fraction of visitors, but don't think of it as smaller in any other way. This enchanting island is still one of the best-kept secrets of the western Mediterranean—perhaps those who love it are deliberately silent.

The island's geography appears simple enough: the capital and biggest town, Mahón (Maó in Menorquí dialect), is at the eastern end, and the former capital Ciutadella lies at the western end. Like a fish's backbone, one main road links them, with places on the north or south coasts connected to it by a mere handful of smaller roads. A detailed map will show a maze of tiny lanes and tracks as well, but, even so, many coves and beaches can be reached only by walking.

The north is greener, lusher, and indented by big bays; the south is a giant rockery, riddled with caves and dotted with prehistoric marvels, its coast a succession of secret coves. Scientists explain the great contrasts between the northern and southern halves in terms of the geological formation of the island.

The Menorquí language includes some words picked up from the British in the 18th century. The subjects, presumably important in relations between the occupiers and the locals, concentrate on carpentry, food, and drink. *Neversó*, for example, is the name of a kind of plum. It comes from a comment made by Sir Richard Kane, the first British governor: "I *never saw* such plums."

 ## Mahón

"The best ports in the Mediterranean—June, July, August, and Mahón," said the 16th-century Venetian admiral Andrea Doria, as he noted that outside the good sailing season of summer, a fleet couldn't do better than shelter here. The 6-km- (4-mile-) long deep-water harbour, guarded by forts at its mouth and shielded from the winds by surrounding hills, caught the eye of the British Royal Navy. In 1708, during the War of the Spanish Succession, they seized the island to have use of the port, and kept possession until temporarily losing it to the French in 1756.

British occupation, on and off until 1802, left its mark. Walk through the older parts of Mahón, and you could almost be in Georgian England. Whole streets, including **Carrer Hannover**, look like 18th-century Portsmouth or Plymouth. Those cities have changed over time, but Mahón has kept its elegant façades and sash windows with their original rippled glass—though, unlike windows in England, those here are usually out of sight behind closed shutters. Some of the old houses are a deep red colour, keeping up a tradition which started when the only paint available was the anti-fouling type for ships.

The historic town of Ciutadella was once Menorca's capital and boasts a 13th-century cathedral.

Mahón is meant for walking: its impenetrable one-way system will threaten your sanity if you try to drive. The little city clusters on the cliffs above the port as well as along the quayside, and near the centre a twisting roadway and flights of broad ceremonial steps lead from one level to the next. At the top level, follow your nose to the **fish market** to see more varieties of octopus and squid than you knew existed. Next to it are the other **markets**, housed in the vast cloisters (*Claustre del Carme*) of a former convent. Look out here for some of Menorca's famous Mahón cheese. Varieties range from the young and mild to a hard-skinned and almost crystalline, long-matured version rivalling the best Parmesan.

The chief landmark in this area is the church of **Santa María**, a large Gothic space under a vaulted roof. It was rebuilt in the 18th century and equipped in 1810 with a massive organ that is still played. The site was occupied by a mosque until 1287, the year the Moors were expelled by Alfonso III. His flattering statue, standing in a little square beside the church, contrives to make a reputedly weak and vicious character look like Sir Galahad. Just round the corner, the stately **Ajuntament** (Town Hall) is graced by a clock presented by Sir Richard (1713–1736). Inside, portraits of Menorcan worthies and French and Spanish governors decorate the walls— there are no British governors, you'll note, though Sir Richard seems to have got on well with the Menorcans and loved the island, devoting himself to improving its agriculture, education, and roads. Good relations between the islanders and the British inevitably turned sour when troops misbehaved and religious arguments blew up, and when later governors busied themselves with lining their own pockets.

A useful direction-finder in Mahón's network of narrow streets is the **Porto Sant Roc**, one of the old city gates (most

You may want to visit the Ajuntament in Mahón to see the portraits of illustrious Menorcans.

of the ramparts having been levelled long ago). Go along the pedestrian streets Carrer Bastió and Carrer de Ses Moreres to the biggest square, **Plaça de S'Esplanada**, which used to be the stage for military parades. Now it's orbited by buses, noisy mopeds, and strollers in the early evening.

Back at the steps leading down to the port, see how the cliffs are riddled with caverns and fortifications. Underneath them, some protected by nets from falling debris, stands an amazing line of disparate old buildings: ramshackle or beautifully restored, from sheds to restaurants.

One legacy from the British to Menorca was a taste for gin. The **Xoriguer distillery**, established in the 18th century, still operates, and you can look through big windows at copper stills bubbling away, producing a hot, colourless spirit which is poured over juniper berries to become gin.

Take a stroll along the quayside to see the variety of vessels tied up here, from battered trawlers to four-masters, and grey ships of the Spanish Navy at their base across the harbour. Continue past the foot of the main steps, and you'll turn the corner into **Cala Figuera** ("English Cove" in the days of the British Navy), where pleasure craft congregate near the ships' chandlers, shops, and restaurants that cater for them.

If you have time, take a **cruise** from Cala Figuera for the best views of Mahón, the harbour islands, and the forts on the shore. Two of the islands once served as quarantine stations, and one was used in the 1820s for training the midshipmen of the U.S. Navy, before the opening of the U.S. Naval Academy at Annapolis, Maryland. This connection developed when American ships were based here during operations against the Barbary pirates of North Africa.

High in the hills of the north side is an imposing pinkish-coloured mansion, Sant Antoní. Part Georgian and part Spanish style, the mansion is better known as **Golden Farm**. Legend has it that Lord Nelson stayed in the house while his ship was in harbour. The house is privately owned, so you'll have to admire it from a distance. Nelson's friend and second-in-command, Admiral Cuthbert Collingwood, who took command when Nelson was killed at Trafalgar, had a house on the southern side of the harbour between Mahón and Es Castell. It is now a charming hotel.

> When visiting churches, shorts, backless dresses and tank tops should not be worn.

Looking out over the harbour mouth toward vast fortifications on the oppositeside (still used as a military base), **Es Castell** (Villacarlos), appears even more English than Mahón. That's not surprising, since under the name of Georgetown it was built as the home of the British Army garrison, whose main task was to man Fort San Felipe by the harbour entrance. The fort was demolished by the Spanish in 1802. The grass-covered foundations and colossal rock-cut caverns are still impressive.

Excursions from Mahón

South and East

Near the city limit, at **Trepucó** on the road south to Sant Lluis, stand Mahón's nearest *talaiot* and *taula*. The site has been damaged, not least when the French army fortified it and mounted guns to fire on the British in Fort San Felipe. However, there are much more magical prehistoric places almost as close to Mahón. For contrasts between the old and new, you can hardly beat **Torelló**, a fine *talaiot* right next to the landing lights at the north end of the airport runway. Topped by the massive stones of a doorway, which suggests that these towers once had upper chambers, it's now crowned with a warning light for aircraft. The site continued in use until early Christian times; the outline of a basilica is visible but mostly fenced off. Not far away is a section of mosaic pavement with peacock and knot motifs. (You'll get here by taking the Sant Climent road from the airport roundabout and very soon turning right down a farm track.)

The colourful Tuesday market takes place on the Plaça de S'Esplanada in Mahón.

Sant Lluis, a strange town of chequerboard streets and all-white houses, was built by the French army as their headquarters in the Seven Years' War (1756–1763). Notice the fine Baroque façade of the church, as well as the whitewashed windmill, restored to working order. The main road bypasses the centre and heads for the handful of resorts dotted round the island's southeast corner.

Small sandy beaches and, in places, rocks to swim from, clear water, and proximity to Mahón and its airport meant that this area was one of the first to be developed for holidays. At S'Algar and Cala d'Alcaufar, villas cluster near a rocky shore, and **Punta Prima** has a sandy but often messy beach. Illa de l'Aire, an island with its lighthouse and its own subspecies of black lizards, lies close by offshore.

Though there's very little to distinguish many of these resorts, **Binibeca Vell** is something different. Inspired by the traditional fishing village, this is an intriguing "toytown" of brilliant white houses and dark wooden beams and shutters. Here and there deep, shaded arches relieve the whiteness. The streets are so narrow that you can touch both sides.

The road makes detours inland on its way west to the resorts of Binidali and Canutells, more usually reached by the direct route from Mahón and the airport. **Cala'En Porter** is one of the largest, oldest-established, and, in season, the loudest holiday towns. All the facilities of a resort are here, and steps lead down to a sandy beach. At **Cova d'En Xoroi** a cave in the steep cliff has been turned into a disco where you can dance above a vertiginous drop to the sea.

In contrast to Cala'En Porter, nearby **Cales Coves** is undeveloped. There's evidence that it was a port in Roman times, although no buildings survive. If you look up at the cliffs, you can see the openings of a hundred and more caves. These were used as burial chambers in the Talaiotic period; today some of them provide shelter for dropouts and backpackers.

Expensive homes on the hillside at Cala Llonga overlook the great harbour. Because the opening of the sea is so narrow and tides are minimal, the water is polluted. Swimmers should head for beaches farther north, at Cala Mesquida and Es Grau.

North Coast

Wild, rocky, and deeply indented, much of the north coast can't be reached by road at all. The excellent main highway from Mahón runs well inland through the gentler landscape of wheat and potato fields and pastures for grazing cattle. The twin coves of Addaia—now a holiday village and harbour—were the site of the last British invasion in 1798, by Scottish Highland troops who probably thought these rocky hillsides covered with purple heather were just like home.

You can drive down to the sea at just a few places, and inevitably some of these have developed rapidly into resorts. **Macaret** was an old fishing village, and much of the new building matches the traditional look, especially around the neat little square. **Arenal d'En Castell** has a beautiful circular bay, almost enclosed and with a wide sandy beach. Intensive construction all round includes high-rise hotels, unusual on Menorca, which generate summer crowds. It's the liveliest place on this side of the island.

Son Parc, with its golf club, villas, shops, and hotel, is a completely artificial creation, near a big, flat sandy beach backed by dunes. By contrast, **Fornells** (which is pronounced "Fornays") was and still is a real fishing village as well as a resort, and has pretty houses and some well-known seafood restaurants lining the waterfront near the entrance to a huge bay. Take a walk up the hill to the old watchtower for a stunning view of the harbour, the coast, and the clearest of blue water. **Ses Salines**, with a sheltered coastline and shallow water, is reckoned to be one of the best places to learn to sail or windsurf.

On the next bay, Cala Fornells (or Platja de Fornells) is one of the best-planned of the newer developments. Its imaginatively designed houses and villas are all different and set amid superb cactus gardens. It shares a beach with the odd-looking Cala Tirant across the water, a small growth of round white villas—one of several Menorcan schemes that ran into difficulties.

If you like geographical extremes, take the rough track to the most northerly point on the island, **Cap de Cavallería**. It's passable by car, with four farm gates to open and close, and leads past the site of the ancient Carthaginian and Roman port of Sanitja, where nothing is to be seen today but a few small boats. At the tip of the narrow headland, walk along the clifftop near the lighthouse for breathtaking views. The remains of gun emplacements date from the Spanish Civil War. Still farther to the west, Binimella is another development that stopped almost before it started, but Menorcans favour its beach at weekends.

West from Mahón

You can do it slowly and make all the stops and side trips, or head straight for the other end of the island. The first could take a day, a week, or a month. The second, less than an hour. Plan to fit the time available.

The busy main road from Mahón to Ciutadella at first runs parallel to the one built by order of the first British governor (named **Camí d'En Kane** in his honour). Farther west, today's road is superimposed on the old route. Near Mahón, you can begin the region's absolute feast of 3,000-year-old megalithic sites.

A few miles from Mahón, a sign to the left points down a lane to **Talatí de Dalt**. Its elegantly slim *taula* has a "supporter" leaning against it, one of the stones that used to form a horseshoe-shaped enclosure and long ago fell into this position. Next to the *taula* is a dark columned room (a "hypostyle court") and, not far away, burial caves. It's a magical spot, especially in the quiet of the early morning or evening.

Back on the main road, a little farther west, keep an eye on the fields on the north side. You're looking for two stone buildings shaped like upturned boats, the *navetas* (or prehistoric burial chambers) at **Rafal**

Tasteful holiday homes overlooking the sea at Binibeca, built to imitate traditional local style.

Rubi Nou. That nearest to the road is in remarkable repair. You have to crawl through the low doorway, but then you'll be surprised at the spacious interior, over 2 metres (7 feet) high, with shelves at each end. The other *naveta* is more of a ruin, but worth seeing for the beautifully recessed stone door frame, evidently designed to take a stone or wooden door.

South of the road, and most easily accessible by the narrow lane from Alaior to Cala'En Porter, **Torralba d'En Salort** has the most beautiful *taula* of all. There's no doubt the ancients here were masters of the art of stone construction.

Try climbing the *talaiot* nearby to get an overview of the whole site, and especially the way the *taula* was set in its horseshoe-shaped sanctuary. There has been some limited restoration here, including the re-erection of some of the smaller standing stones. Recent excavations and radiocarbon dating put the *taula*'s date at about 900 B.C.

At the next crossroads to the south, heading towards Cala'En Porter, turn west and you'll reach a farm where the owner has painted red arrows to direct you to another remarkable site, **Torre Llisa Vell**. Here you can make a dramatic entry into the *taula* precinct through the original doorway. Back on the Cala En Porter road, head south for about .5 km (⅓ mile) and you'll see on your right the two enormous *talaiots* of **Sonacasana**, where recent excavation has revealed a whole complex of buildings.

Alaior, white houses clustered on a low hill, looks at a distance almost like an Arab village. Take the time to go to the top of the town and see its most attractive quarter. A long, sandy, gently sloping beach and sand dunes have brought obtrusive hotel and villa developments to the south coast at Sant Jaume and Son Bou. As well as waterslides and windsurfers, you can see here the outline of a fifth-century basilica discovered in 1951, next to the beach at its eastern end.

A turning off the Alaior–Son Bou road, signposted to **Torre d'En Gaumés**, brings you to the biggest, most varied —and most confusing—of the prehistoric settlements. Don't miss the hypostyle court, with its central supports and massive roof intact, or the water cisterns carved out in the soft sandstone rock. Shallow dishes cut in the flat stone may have been used for settling debris out of the water before running it into the cisterns.

The south coast lacks the big inlets of the north, but it's rugged and cut by river valleys, so here, too, no road follows the shore for any great distance. Beach resorts may be almost adjoining, but if you want to drive from one to the other, it can mean a long detour back to the main road.

Choose a clear day, and then head off for Mercadal, halfway along the main east–west highway. Here, climb the twisting but well-contoured road to the top of **Monte Toro**, Menorca's highest peak. It's only 357 metres (1,171 feet) high, but it stands up so sharply that it provides the best view of the whole island.

> **Full tank, please -**
> *llénelo, por favor.*
> (**lyay**nayloa por fahb**hor**)

A horseshoe-shaped cove with white sand and turquoise water sheltered by cliffs and green pine woods has made the stunningly beautiful **Cala Santa Galdana** one of Menorca's most popular holiday destinations. The main hotel is somewhat obtrusive, but trees hide many of the other building excesses. Escape some of the crowds by taking the half-hour's walk west along forest paths to the pretty cove of **Macarella**. The even lovelier **Macarelleta** (a nudist beach) is a further ten minutes' walk or a swim away. Both have been used from the earliest times: in places you'll be using prehistoric steps cut into the rock. The coves can also be reached from the west by car along rough unmarked tracks.

A few miles west of Ferreríes, north of the cross-island road, is a climb to the hilltop ruins of the **castle of Santa Agueda**. The track forks right from a narrow lane heading north and climbs steeply. In places the path is only just passable on foot; then it suddenly widens into a beautifully paved Roman road. Not much is left of the old castle, or the farm within the ramparts.

Ciutadella

"Little city," the name means, and until the early 18th century Ciutadella was the capital of Menorca. It was the British who made the change, as they were on the island mainly for Mahón's harbour, and Ciutadella's beautiful but narrow and shallow inlet could not compete.

The two cities are so unalike it's difficult to believe they are hardly 45 km (28 miles) apart. The difference, however, is essentially in the atmosphere rather than in the architecture. Mahón means business, but Ciutadella displays a gentler mood, remarkably unaffected by its summer visitors. There aren't many hotels—the resorts are out of town to the north and south.

Plaça Alfons III now marks the spot where the road from Mahón reached the old city gates. The gates are long gone, but the cafés around the square probably began life by refreshing thirsty travellers. Stroll along the main street that bisects the old part of the city. It takes various different names, starting here as Carrer de Maó and at Sa Plaça Nova becoming Carrer J M Quadrado, one side of which, the lovely **Ses Voltes**, is completely arcaded in Moorish style. Everywhere shops and restaurants are ingeniously and discreetly fitted in.

There's much wonderful stonework, its honey colour turning to gold as the sun goes down. Look especially for the carved doorway of **Església del Rosari** across from the cathedral down the side street Carrer del Rosari. The **cathedral**, begun in the 13th century, has been modified over the centuries. The bishop's palace adjoins it.

The main street brings you to **Plaça d'es Born**, the ceremonial square on the heights above the harbour. Formerly the Moors' parade ground, it is lined with imposing buildings, such as the former Ajuntament (now the police headquarters) and great 19th-century mansions. In the middle of the square, an obelisk commemorates a brave defence against some 15,000 besieging Turks in 1558. The town fell after nine days, and the survivors were carried off into slavery.

In the **port**, a long curving inlet is lined with fishing boats on one side and pleasure craft on the other. Morning and evening you can watch the fishermen return with their catches. Many fish travel only as far as restaurants on the water-

MENORCA: BEACH HIGHLIGHTS

For beaches on Mallorca, see page 71.

Cala Presili: Two remote beaches, Platja de Capifort and Platja d'En Tortuga, both with fine and rough sand, transparent water, and good snorkelling. Road access is difficult: a track leads over rocks from the Cap de Favaritx. No facilities.

Cala Pregonda: Breathtaking scenery, sandy beaches, and rocky islands in a protected area. Reached by a path from Platja Binimella. No facilities.

Algaiarens: A fine sandy beach, with crystal-clear water, in an area of outstanding natural beauty, La Vall. The beach is a short walk away from the car park (a small charge is payable).

Cala En Turqueta–Cala Macarella: Two popular coves, with fine sand and brilliant blue water. Road access is from Oratorio de Sant Joan de Missa—take the right-hand lane for Cala En Turqueta, the left-hand lane for Cala Macarella. Beach bar facilities.

front, some housed in caverns in the base of the harbour bastion and expanding onto the quay on warm nights. Bars and discos make this area the focus of Ciutadella nightlife.

It may seem strange to find a statue of the American Civil War hero Admiral David Farragut on the southern edge of town near the second, smaller inlet. His father was born on the island and emigrated to the United States. The first admiral of the U.S. Navy was declared an honorary Menorcan.

☞ Prehistory near Ciutadella

Some 5 km (3 miles) from the city, just to the south of the main road, stands the **Naveta d'Es Tudons**, not to be missed. A burial chamber claimed as the oldest roofed building in Europe, it dates from around 1000 B.C. As you'll see when you crawl through the tiny entrance, the burial chamber is a double-decker, and has a small anteroom where you can stand upright and enter either floor. When it was excavated in the 1950s and again in the 1970s, many bones were found, along with some bronze ornaments. Restoration work done at the same time is the explanation for the pristine condition of the chamber. Overall, it measures 14 metres (46 feet) in length, approximately 6.5 metres (21 feet) in width, and up to 4 metres (13 feet) in height. Notice the massive slabs that form the twin roofs: not having devised the true arch, the ancients could utilize stone with this method to make a large room.

Two intriguing *taula* sites are hidden not far away. Heading away from Ciutadella, just after Naveta d'Es Tudons take the next lane to the south, and after 2.5 km (1½ miles) turn left down a farm track to Torre Trencada. There is a signpost pointing across the fields to the *taula* and a huge cave. Back on the main road, take the next turning south, through stone gateposts and across a farmyard, to the largely unexcavated **Torre Llafuda**, obscured by trees. From the *talaiot* there's a wonderful view of the strange countryside around.

Head out of Ciutadella on the road towards Sant Joan de Missa and branch off towards Son Saura; after 6 km (4 miles) you'll arrive at the prehistoric walled town of **Son Catlar**, which is situated in the farmland to the east of the road. Ask the farmer politely if you may look round. You can walk round the 900-metre- (2,880-foot-) long walls, which possibly date from about 600 B.C., though on the southeastern side you can see places where, much later, the Romans built bastions. The *taula* seems to have been deliberately broken off, and it is possible that the Romans used the precinct as a temple. North of Ciutadella, on the road to Punta Nati, turn right at the old car dump and you'll come to the *talaiots* of **Torre Vella**. The most northerly one has its entrance and a large interior room intact.

Clear blue seas and white houses form a typical Mediterranean scene at Port de Ciutadella.

Beaches and Resorts near Ciutadella

Almost every accessible cove and inlet on the coast near Ciutadella has been developed in a rash of *urbanizaciónes*, creating a great number of holiday homes, hotels, and associated facilities, but the total effect tends to be dull and suburban. Beaches here are very small, and overcrowded in high summer.

To the south of the city, Santandria's narrow sandy beach can be dirty. Most of the coastline is made up of sharp rocks,

Mysterious Megaliths

Being on Menorca can sometimes feel like being on the set of the "Flintstones"—so much is made out of stone: dog kennels, drinking troughs for cattle, neat flights of projecting steps set into stone walls wherever you need to climb over. All those walls represent millennia of superhuman effort by a population that in ancient times can never have numbered more than a few thousand. But Menorca's stonemasons did far more: they created remarkable buildings, hundreds of towers called *talaiots*, and burial chambers, or *navetas*, in the shape of upturned boats. The uniquely Menorcan *taula*, a massive T-shape made of two blocks of

subtly carved stone, was their masterpiece. We can only guess how they handled such weights. What were they for? Some have suggested that they held up a sort of roof structure, or that sacrifices or the bodies of the dead were exposed on top. Now it's more generally accepted that a *taula* was the focus of a religious cult, the centrepiece of a temple.

but when you do find a spot to swim from, the water here is clear and enticing—perfect for snorkelling. Cala Blanca, with its huge white hotel and many apartments, gets especially crowded. At the windswept southwestern corner of the island, Cap d'Artrutx has been heavily built up, but fortunately the rules have ensured that construction is back 100 metres (320 feet) from the sea. East of the cape, **Cala en Bosç** has a sheltered harbour, with an attractive marina and sports facilities.

Farther to the east, the sea is reached only by narrow lanes and farm tracks, but local people and regular visitors reckon it's worth a trek to get away from the crowds. Occasionally there are times when so many head for the remote spots that they create a crowd there, too. One of their favourites is **Cala Turqueta**, reached from Ciutadella by the Sant Joan de Missa road. Another spot, Son Saura, down the lane past Son Catlar, involves opening and closing eight farm gates along a potholed dirt track. It's a chance to see rural Menorca, but the beach can be covered with heaps of dry weed, and you may not think it worth the effort.

Just west of Ciutadella, Cala Blanes and the vast area of villas and hotels near Cala Forcat make a self-contained holiday town, though their two often scruffy little beaches can hardly cope with the summer influx.

The northwest corner of the island, in total contrast, is almost untouched by tourism, and environmentalists want it declared a no-go area for development. Some building at **Cala Morell** has jumped the gun, and a number of little white houses and blocks of villas have sprouted on the eastern side of one of the loveliest bays on the north coast. A maze of paths leads down to the rocky shore and around the cliffs, a geology textbook of tortured strata. You'll be tempted to swim from the ledges here, but beware of treading on the spiny sea urchins.

WHAT TO DO

SPORTS

To get in, on, or under the water is the aim of most summer visitors, and both Mallorca and Menorca can offer just about every known method. The mild climate of the islands provides a longer season for sports ashore, with a mass of other diversions and many activities that children will enjoy as a break from the beach.

Many hotels as well as villa or apartment complexes have their own tennis and squash courts. Despite these increased facilities, you frequently have to book a day ahead. You pay by the hour, and may be able to hire rackets and take lessons at the bigger resorts and clubs. Ranches (*ranchos*) and stables are scattered over both islands, so you can hire a mount and go off horseback riding. For more information, contact the Club Escuela de Equitación de Mallorca, tel. 61 31 57. Go-karting fans will find circuits at Magalluf and Ca'n Picafort. Anyone feeling more adventurous can take off in a micro-light from the fields near Cap Blanc and Campos, or hang-glide from the mountaintops. Tourist information offices have details.

Swimming. Gently sloping expanses of sand, rocks to dive off into deep water, sheltered bay, or open sea: the choice is enormous, so try to find out what the beach is like before you choose your resort. For learning to windsurf (boardsail), choose somewhere with plenty of shallow water (such as Ses Salines on Menorca). That will also suit small children in your party, but keep an eye on them just the same in the summer crowds. Although lifeguards are rare, the larger beaches do have first-aid stations. Just a few more words of warning: beware of spiky sea urchins when swimming off rocks; and remember the sun is still burning you when you're in the

Alcúdia Aqua Park is high on the list of Mallorcan attractions — for children and adults alike.

water, even though you can't feel it. Take along plenty of protective sunscreen — up as high as Factor 28.

Boating and sailing. Escape the crowds and sail to an idyllic deserted cove. That's the object of thousands who keep their own boats here all year round. You can get away from it all, as well, by hiring various sorts of craft for an hour, day, or week, at many beaches and hotels (but note that you will be required to produce a valid qualification for a self-drive motor boat). The stately "pedalo" for two won't go fast, and it's stable enough for adults to take small children with them. If you want to try out a sailing dinghy, lessons are available for complete novices in order to get them started. There are also windsurfing (boardsailing) schools, and you can find boards to hire and conditions to suit everyone.

Snorkelling and diving. Take your mask and flippers — the water is crystal clear, especially off rocks and away from near-landlocked harbours. To spear-fish you need a licence, and must be 200 metres (650 feet) or more from the beach. Scuba-diving equipment is for hire, if you have a qualification from your home country. To obtain this diploma during your holiday, you can take a five-day series of lessons, usually starting in a hotel pool and graduating to supervised dives to a depth of 12 metres (39 feet).

Waterskiing. This is expensive, especially if you're taking lessons. Try to negotiate a big discount if you intend to water-ski a lot. Designation of areas for different water sports is not always enforced or clear, so expect to encounter both swimmers and craft. If you are swimming, try to make yourself obvious, and keep out of areas in which powerboats and jet-skis are operating.

Tee off early at one of Mallorca's ten challenging golf courses.

Fishing. Locals and visitors alike enjoy fishing from rocky shores and harbour jetties. Some experts say there's a greater chance of a making a catch in the cooler days of spring and autumn, and in the hours after sunset. To fish from a boat, obtain a licence from the Commandancia de Marina, Moll Muelle Viejo s/n, Palma, tel. 71 13 71, and for freshwater fishing in the reservoirs of Gorg Blau and Pla de Cúber, obtain a permit from SECONA, Passatge de Guillermo de Torrela, 1, Palma, tel. 71 74 40.

Walking. Pure pleasure—and it's literally the only way to go if you want to reach some of the hilltop castles and remoter stretches of coast. April and May, with a wild profusion of flowers, are reckoned to be the best walking time. In the hotter months, start early or make use of the long evenings. On Mallorca the mountains of the northwest make for the most dramatic scenery, to be seen on the climb to Castell d'Alaró (see page 41) as well as between the Monastery of Lluc and the coast. Reserve a Saturday for the walk to the Castell del Rei near Pollença (see page 44). On Menorca, search for more elusive prehistoric sites, take the cliff paths of the northwest or south coasts, or climb to Santa Agueda (see page 69). There are a number of other good walks in a leaflet published by the Balearic Government Tourist Office, at Avinguda del Rei Jaume III, 10, Palma. Wear sturdy rubber-soled shoes for climbing over rocks.

Golf. There are ten golf courses on the island, three of which are 9-hole, the rest 18-hole. All are varied and challenging enough for the best players. You can also hire equipment and take lessons. Beautifully landscaped Son Vida hosts the Balearics' Open, while Santa Ponça's 10th hole, at 590 metres (1,966 feet), is one of Europe's longest. Tee off early: at times, you'll spend a lot of time waiting for players ahead of you. Menorca has a 9-hole course at Son Parc on the north coast, and another in the southeast. For further information, contact the Federación Balear de Golf, Avinguda del Rei Jaume III, 17, Palma, tel. 72 27 53.

Cycling. In the spring, thousands of serious cyclists come to Mallorca from all over Europe, and tear all over the island in races and time trials or grind up the steepest mountain passes just for the fun of it. Summer tourists make gentler progress on the bikes they've hired at the resorts. It's a wonderful way to get around. If you're going to join in, check the brakes and tyres and make sure a strong lock is included.

Bird-watching. The islands' resident birds would be enticing enough, but it's the visiting species that generate most excitement. Migrants from Africa stop to rest in the Balearics, and some stay for the summer. Birds of prey rare elsewhere in Europe are spotted here, and stretches of water, which include S'Albufera and Salines de Llevant on Mallorca, and S'Albufera on Menorca, attract waterfowl.

Spectator sports. As this is Spain, you'll expect there to be **bullfights**. They're staged on summer Sunday afternoons in Palma's big bullring (Plaça de Toros), and less regularly at Inca and Muro. (Menorca has no bullfights.) If you've never seen the *corrida*, be prepared to witness an ancient ritual; you may come to understand why aficionados regard it as an art form. Choose your seat carefully: *sol* means you'll be in the full heat and dazzle of the sun, at least at first. The more expensive *sombra* means shade, so *sol y sombra* means, logically that you'll get some of each, though the sun won't be in your eyes.

Less controversial, **trotting races** are held every Sunday, all the year round, at the tracks (*Hipodròm*) at Son Pardo near Palma and Manacor, and near Mahón and Ciutadella. The informal atmosphere and casual-looking handicap starts can be deceptive. The competition is fierce, and foreign owners and horses are involved. Betting is organized through a centralized "tote" system.

If you fancy your chances of picking winning **greyhounds**, head for Palma's *Canodròm*, Camí de Jesús, where they run several times a week.

FOLKLORE AND FESTIVALS

Hand-in-hand with the revival of the island languages, a renewed interest in Balearic culture has taken place. Children learn many traditional dances, and shows are put on by **folk dance** troupes at the resorts as well as during fiestas. The oldest of the dances are survivals from Moorish times, and are usually performed in mountain villages: in *els cossiers*, groups move together to the rhythm of drums and the sound of the tambourine and shawm (an ancient form of oboe). Dances are held in Algaida on 25 July and 16 August and in Montuiri on 24 July and 15, 23, and 24 August. The dance of *els cavallets* is performed in Pollença on 2 August at the Dia de la Patrona, and in Felanitx on 20 July and again on the Dia de San Augustine on 28 August. Another dance, the *parado*, resembles a courtly minuet: it is performed in Valldemossa in the square beside the monastery. The distinctive dances of Menorca include the *ball d'es cossil*, which is thought to be derived from Scottish dancing. The dance, something like the English maypole dance, is performed during the fiesta in Es Migjorn Gran.

Major Music Festivals

Summer festivals of classical music are held from July to September; further information can be obtained by calling the numbers given below.

Festival of Deià: San Marroig and parish church of Deià; tel. 63 91 78

Frédéric Chopin Festival: Sa Cartuja, Valldemossa; tel. 61 23 51

Festival of Pollença: Cloister of Santo Domingo Convent; tel. 53 06 69

Festival de Musica d'Estiu de Ciutadella: held in the cloister of the seminary, Ciutadella; tel. 38 41 23

International Classical Music Festival: Santa Maria Church, Mahón; tel. 35 23 08 or 15 12 09

FESTIVALS

Saints' days, holidays, and *fiestas* are so frequent in Mallorca and Menorca that the chances are good that at least one will coincide with your stay.

5 Jan: *Procession of the Magi,* all towns and villages. In Palma the Three Kings arrive by boat, amid noisy rejoicing, and give out presents in Plaça Cort.

16/17 Jan: *Sant Antoní,* patron of animals. Bonfires, dancing, and singing during the evening of the 16th, best in Sa Pobla, Pollença, and Artà. On the 17th lively processions for the blessings of the animals, best in Palma, Artà, Pollença, Muro, and Son Severa. In Pollença the Pi de Ternelles is climbed in the late afternoon near the parish church.

20 Jan: *San Sebastián,* patron saint of Palma. A week of concerts, exhibitions, and events. The night before is *Revetla,* with dancing and music in the Plaza Mayor.

Feb: *Carnaval.* Fancy dress and masked balls, culminating in *Sa Rua,* a colourful procession through the streets of Palma on the Sunday before Lent.

March/April: Holy Week processions in most towns. Best in Pollença, Artà, Palma, Sineu, and Deià.

May (2nd week): Sóller celebrates a great victory over pirate raiders in 1561.

23-24 June: *Sant Joan* (St. John). A week of fiestas in Muro, Ciutadella, Sant Joan, and Deià.

29 June: *San Pere,* patron of fishermen. Sea processions, open-air dances, grilled fish, bread, and wine. Best are Colònia de San Pedro, Palma, Alcúdia, Sóller, and Andraitx.

15-16 July: *Virgen de Carme.* Processions of decorated boats and open-air dancing; best in Porto Colom, Port de Sóller (at dusk), Mahón, and Fornells.

24-26 July: *San Jaume* (St. James). Street processions, open-air dancing, bullfights, and daytime events; best are in Alcúdia, Palma, Inca, Muro, Es Castell (Villacarlos), and devil-dances in Algaida.

27-28 July: *Santa Catalina Thomàs.* Procession of decorated carts in Valldemossa, and concert in the monastery.

30 July: *San Abdon and San Senen,* Inca. Concerts, folk-dancing, bullfights, and fireworks.

2 Aug: *Patrona de Pollença.* A week of celebrations, dancing, exhibitions, fireworks, and a craft show in the cloister of Santo Domingo. Pollença also stages a mock battle between Moors and Christians through the streets.

Aug: *Three International Music Festivals,* including concerts in Palma in the wonderful cloisters of Sant Frances; in Pollença in the cloister of Santo Domingo; and Deià in Son Marroig and Deià parish church. (See page 81)

11-13 Aug: *Patrona de Alaior y San Llorenc.* Song Festival, concerts, and traditional equestrian events.

Aug (last Sun): *Patrona de Sant Lluis.* Parades, music, and an interesting craft fair.

7, 8, 9 Sept: *Nativity of the Virgin.* Processions, folk events in many places. *Dia de la Patrona de Mahón.* Three days of festivities, including equestrian events.

End Sept: *Binissalem Wine Festival.* A week of fiesta, music, dancing, fireworks, processions, and, of course, winetasting.

Oct (first Sun): *Festa d'es Butifarra,* Sant Joan. Gastronomic festival with free sampling of cured meats and sausages.

31 Oct: *Eve of All Saints' Day.* Rosaries made of *panallets* and *carabassat* (local sweets) are given to children.

Nov (2nd Thurs): *Dijous Bo* or "Good Thursday." Largest agricultural fair of the island at Inca—folk dancing, competitions, exhibitions, and an enormous street market.

Nov-Dec: *Agricultural fairs,* many inland towns. Best are Pollença and Sa Pobla.

31 Dec: *Festa de Standa.* Palma celebrates the liberation of the city from Moorish rule in 1229 with a Royal Standard procession through the streets.

SHOPPING

Shopping Hours

Most stores are open from 9:00 A.M. to 1:00 or 1:30 P.M. and again from 4:30 or 5:00 to 8:00 P.M. The hours in between are devoted to lunch and the siesta. The big department stores and hypermarkets of Palma defy the tradition by remaining open all the day. In summer, the shops in the resorts may be open until 10:00 P.M. Practically everywhere will be closed on Sundays.

Best Buys

Mallorca and Menorca alike are famous for their **leather**: well-known makes of shoes sold in Paris or Italy are quite likely to have come from the islands. So does some of the finest leather and suede clothing, much of it from factories in Inca, which you can visit. You're welcome in the factory retail outlets there, and at Ciutadella and Alaior on Menorca. Although such places have signs saying "factory prices," these may not be much lower than in the stores of Palma—a lot of the products on sale won't have come from that factory in any case. The prices should, however, be significantly less than in your home country, and less than in mainland Spain.

> **Signs:**
> *rebajas* - sale

While you admire the quality of the very best leather—it can seem as supple as silk—do check for flaws and look at the stitching. Some of the items are "seconds": that may be why they are here. You may be able to negotiate discounts.

Mallorcan **artificial pearls**, manufactured in Manacor (see page 56), are exported in great numbers. They're a good buy; prices do not vary much from shop to shop. There may be a small saving at the factory showroom, and it's here you'll have the biggest choice.

Wines and many other **alcoholic drinks** are still cheap by the standards of the rest of Europe. This applies especially to foreign brands made under license in Spain. Cuban **cigars** are priced at significantly less than you would pay elsewhere in western Europe.

Souvenirs

A few of the "souvenir supermarkets" along the main roads, near some of the tourist attractions of Mallorca, will give you an idea of what is available. It seems that everything "Spanish" ever devised for the tourist trade is piled high here, from charming craftwork to laughable junk. But don't assume that you will find the best prices in this sort of place. They are intended to cater for excursion parties. The smaller tourist-oriented shops, as well, aren't likely to offer the best prices. Check prices, but then look elsewhere, including in street mar-

Specimens of colourful glassware are among the local crafts available as souvenirs.

kets. **Embroidered linen** can be attractive. So can handmade **baskets** (although some come from China) and **glass** items. Authentically Mallorcan are the weird pottery figures called *siurells,* painted in red and green on white. Similar relics have been around since Phoenician times. They have a spoutlike whistle, and rather phallic versions are not just a modern joke: fertility is part of the *siurell* lore.

Shopping Tips

Because Palma overshadows everywhere else on Mallorca in the scale and sophistication of its shops, the other towns scarcely try to compete. So it's to the capital you'll have to go if you're looking for a wide choice. Some of the most fashion-

---

Market Days

The same sellers move with their goods from town to town, so markets don't vary much. All but the smallest places have one, on the same day each week and usually in the morning (as shown below, except where marked "pm").

Sunday	Alcúdia, Felanitx, Inca (flea market), Lluchmajor, Muro, Sa Pobla, Pollença, Santa María.
Monday	Calvia, Manacor.
Tuesday	Alcúdia, Artà, Lluchmajor, Santa Margalida, Mahón.
Wednesday	Andraitx, Capdepera, Colònia Sant Jordi, Port de Pollença, Sineu.
Thursday	Alaior, Campos, Inca, S'Arenal, Ses Salines.
Friday	Alaro (pm), Algaida, Binissalem, Santa Eugenia, Son Servera.
Saturday	Bunyola, Cala Ratjada, Ciutadella, Palma (with fleamarket), Sóller (with flea market).

---

able shops are on Avinguda del Rei Jaume III. Look out for jewellery along Carrer Plateria, and try Carrer Jaume II for clothing and fans. Plaça Major holds a craft market every Friday and Saturday. On Menorca, both Mahón and Ciutadella provide smaller but attractive pedestrianized shopping areas.

Ask for a discount if you're paying by cash—and even if you aren't. But don't expect to be able to bargain, except discreetly in the antiques shops and in the open-air markets. The value-added tax (IVA) imposed on most goods can be refunded on major purchases if you are exporting them. To obtain the rebate, you simply fill in a form provided by the shop where you purchase the goods. One copy is kept by the shop; the other three must be presented at customs on your departure, with the goods. The rebate is forwarded to you at your home address.

ENTERTAINMENT

The bigger the resort, the more varied the activities. There's something for everyone.

Discos, of course—you will probably be offered tickets to buy while you're lying on the beach, or even free ones if the owners are trying to boost a place, or if the *tiquetero* thinks that your good looks will be an asset. **Bars** everywhere: local, French, British, Scandinavian, and German décors, accents, and beers; huge or cosy, with meals, snacks, or nothing; pool tables or a dance floor; loud music or loud TVs.

Films are usually screened dubbed into Spanish, with rare exceptions in the biggest resorts. Islanders have taken to video rental, and though most stocks are natually in Spanish, there are some in English where the foreign population is concentrated.

Bigger package **hotels** boast entertainers operating in two or three languages to ginger up the older crowd with competitions, sing-alongs, and a more sedate sort of dancing.

Hotels sometimes organize **flamenco** nights; even though these songs and dances come from Andalusia, they have become a feature of holidays in many other parts of Spain. The shows are more or less authentic, with singers, dancers and guitarists, though they tend to concentrate on the more cheerful *cante chico* (or light song) rather than the slow, sobbingly emotional *cante jondo* (song of the soul).

The **dinner-and-show excursions** widely on offer include more flamenco, cabaret, and striptease. At the Casino de Mallorca, depending on the package you opt for, you'll get dinner, house wines, and entry into the gaming rooms (you'll need to show your passport) to try your luck at roulette, blackjack, craps, and slot machines. The show typically doesn't finish until the small hours, so be sure to take a siesta beforehand.

> **¡ A su salud! - Cheers!**

Medieval nights hosted by a wicked count, pirates, barbecues with folk dancing; there's something different here every night if you have the stamina.

CHILDREN'S MALLORCA AND MENORCA

Fine sandy beaches and sunny weather make the islands an ideal family destination. If the beach or pool begins to pall, kids can make a bigger splash on a giant waterslide. **Aquacity** at S'Arenal claims to be the biggest aquatic park in the world. Others are at Magalluf, Alcúdia, and Sant Jaume on Menorca. The staff are safety-conscious, so parents can relax at the park's pools and cafés. The larger parks are quite expensive, so plan a long stay to get your money's worth. More sedate is **Marineland**, west of Palma at Costa d'En Blanes, featuring dolphins, performing parrots, and sea lions.

A boat **excursion** is excellent for children. Boats link all the resorts fringing the Bay of Palma, from S'Arenal to Portals Vells—use them like a bus service. From Port de Pollença or Port d'Alcúdia, try a cruise round the cliffs of Cap de Formentor. Sailings from Port de Sóller go to the rugged northwest coast. Trips from Colònia de Sant Jordi/Campos land at the strange isle of Cabrera (see page 53). Enquire about summer schedules between Port d'Alcúdia and Ciutadella, Menorca. A cruise round the historic harbour of Mahón (Maó) on Menorca is also fun.

You'll see rhinos, ostriches and antelopes living happily in the **Reserva Africana** (see page 48), a small Safari Park near Cala Millor. Visitors can drive through as slowly as they like or ride on an open waggon.

Older children will appreciate **La Granja** near Esporles (see page 35). On this beautiful old country estate you can see craftspeople working and lively folk dance displays.

The old-style **trains** going between Palma and Sóller (see page 39) are bound to be popular with children of all ages. Mallorca's other line, from Palma to Inca, is not so picturesque, but it's a fun way of reaching Inca's Thursday market.

Balloons in all different colours, shapes, and sizes, to bring a smile to any child's face.

EATING OUT

In the Balearics you could live entirely on "fast food" or Italian, German, or English cuisine served at beach cafés and resort restaurants. Many hotels seem to be convinced—probably from past experience—that a bland international diet is what visitors want, rather than any indigenous dishes. You'll frequently be served buffets of various salads and hot and cold dishes—the same you've always eaten at home. As a gesture towards "Spanishness," paella is widely offered, and although this combination of saffron rice with permutations of seafood, onion, garlic, pork, rabbit, peppers and peas can be delicious, it's a traditional lunch dish from Valencia, not the islands. Gazpacho, the cold and zesty "liquid salad" soup, is yet another import, coming from Andalusia.

Fortunately, there's a different world awaiting. To enter it, you have simply to find out where the islanders themselves

*Pavement cafés and meals al fresco are among
the great pleasures of Mediterranean life.*

like to eat—our list of recommended eating establishments on page 136 will give you a head start. Try the villages, including the ones near Palma, and the inland towns (such as Inca—well known for its restaurants). Look for unpretentious places and half-hidden cellars. As for what to eat, read on.

Local Specialities

There's a wonderful variety of dishes to sample, arising from the different waves of influence that, from time to time, overtook the Balearics. However, remember that for centuries, people here were poor. Their history is reflected in the simple and robust peasant fare made from the healthiest ingredients. The food can be filling—that was the intention—and helpings tend to be enormous (some places will serve half-portions—*media-ración*).

Pa amb oli, literally bread with oil, has now evolved into a range of open sandwiches. Country bread is spread with a little olive oil, perhaps rubbed with sun-dried tomatoes and topped with olives or capers. Today's more opulent versions are loaded with cheese or the excellent local ham.

Sopas Mallorquínas—in the plural form, as it is shown on menus—is something between a soup and a stew, a combination of vegetables (including cauliflower, onion, whatever's in season), olives, and a little garlic, presented with slices of bread to soak up the juices. Fancier versions may include pork and mushrooms. They're all served

> **Enjoy your meal! -
> *¡Buen provecho!***
> (bwayn pro**vaych**oh)

in an earthenware platter, or *greixonera de terra*, which in turn gave its name to a complete range of stews: *greixonera de peix*, a fish stew, and *greixonera d'aubergínies* (or *berenjenas* in Castilian), a mouthwatering preparation of aubergines (eggplant).

The islanders' liking for a "fry-up" wasn't acquired from the British. Because of the easy availability of olive oil, it was only natural to use it to sauté whatever came to hand. *Tumbet* is a combination of peppers, aubergines, tomatoes, and potatoes cooked in oil, and *frit Mallorquí*, a tasty concoction of strips of fried liver, kidney, peppers, leeks, and other optional extras.

In the past, self-sufficiency was the watchword. The habit dies hard, and after rain you'll still see people out at night carrying lights. They're looking for snails, or *caracoles*, which turn up on many menus, served with a garlic mayonnaise. Another once abundant free supply of protein, rabbit (*conejo*), appears in traditional stews. Especially on Mallorca, every rural family kept pigs, and many still do. So pork and all its by-products are a mainstay, including hams and bacons, *botifarró* (a spicy blood sausage) and *lechona asada*, roast sucking pig, which is really a Christmas dish but features year-round on menus.

Mallorca's *sobrasada*—its justly famous sausage made of pork and red peppers (the mild variety)—is something of an acquired taste. Try some: you may love it, and even eat it with honey, in the local way. The combining of sweet and savoury flavours, and putting almonds in stews, may date from the time of the Moors (although they would not have eaten any pork). *Zarzuela de mariscos*, for example, contains shellfish, tomatoes, garlic, wine, and almonds. Look out for seasonal savoury pies—some being the speciality of just one particular town; *espinagada,* which is an eel-and-spinach pie, is popular in Sa Pobla, while *panades de peix* (fish pies) should be savoured in San Joan.

Crème caramel (or *flan*) is as curiously universal on the Balearics as the mainland, but you ought to be able to find some sweet pastries and pies or some of the almond and honey desserts that are a delicious legacy of the Moors. Vegetarians should be aware, however, that even in confectionery lard (*saim*) is an essential Mallorcan ingredient.

As you drive through inland towns (such as Vilafranca de Bonany) in the late afternoon, watch out for women seated at their front doors selling *bunyelos*. These are bite-sized round doughnuts, deep-fried in lard and then dipped in sugar. Who knows, the Mallorcans may be the inventors of the doughnut. After all, some of them claim Christopher Columbus.

Fish

People coming to islands naturally expect to eat plenty of fish. Here, they still can, but at a price. Stocks in the Mediterranean have become depleted and the local fishermen cannot keep up with the demand, especially in summer. Supplies ei-

Island Differences

Although many dishes are common to both isles, don't be surprised to find big variations between Mallorca and Menorca. Their distinctive histories and the smaller island's colder, windier winters led to differences in crops and customs. Menorcan cooks use more cream, butter and cheese, and correspondingly less olive oil, though they do make a simple soup called oliaigua, "oil and water" (it contains eggs too!).

Vestiges of English in the Menorquí language hint at words introduced during the periods of British rule— *púdins, píquels, and grevi*—but it's a French word that has carried Menorca around the gastronomic world. A running battle continues over the exact origin, but there's little doubt that mayonnaise is named after Mahón. One story has it that the sauce was concocted in Paris, and named in honour of the French victory of 1756 over the English. Menorcans will have none of that: they believe it's a local invention, made famous when it was served to the Duc de Richelieu during the French occupation.

This is what holidays are for: sit and relax with a drink while your food is prepared on a charcoal grill.

ther have to be brought from Spain's Atlantic ports—and they're expensive—or frozen (and sometimes unfortunately both). *Salmonete* is red mullet, which *is* caught locally. So are some of the *langostas*, spiny lobsters which are found on many a menu and are a big attraction in the fish restaurants of Fornells on the north coast of Menorca. *Caldereta de langosta* is a tasty lobster stew. *Merluza*, a Spanish standby, is hake, and *bacalao* is cod—frequently salted and dried, and not suited to everyone's taste. Farmed trout (*trucha*) and sole (*lenguado*) are imported into the islands frozen, and feature on many cheaper menus.

Restaurants and Menus

Spanish restaurants are officially graded from one to five forks, the latter being the most elegant. Forks are awarded for facilities and menu size, however, which may have little to do with the quality of the food.

Many offer a *menú del día*, a daily set menu. (If you ask for the "menu," the waiter will probably think the set meal is what you mean. If you actually want to look at the full list of dishes available, ask for *la carta* or *la lista de platos*.) For a fixed price, you'll get three courses: soup or salad, main dish (with a small choice), and dessert (ice-cream, a piece of fruit or pastry), plus wine, beer, or bottled water. Typically, the cost is about one-third of what you'd expect to pay if you ordered from the regular menu. Many restaurants only have a *menú del día* at lunchtime, but if you are on a budget, don't be reluctant to ask if there is one, anywhere, any time. No place worth its salt should make you feel uncomfortable for choosing their "day's special."

Incidentally, most prices include service, but it's customary to leave something extra.

Bars and Cafés

These establishments are an important institution in Spanish life. Some are open at first light to cater for early-morning workers; nearly all are open by 8:30 PM for breakfast. Open-air cafés are justifiably popular with tourists. One of the great pleasures of the Mediterranean is sitting outside in the early morning with a *café con leche* (white coffee) and watching a town come to life. The price of a coffee also buys you a seat at a table for as long as you care to sit there.

While sitting in a café or bar you might be approached by either lottery-ticket vendors or flower-sellers. If you are not interested in what they offer, simply say *no, gracias*.

Wines and spirits are served at all hours in bars and cafés. It's usually 10 to 15 per cent cheaper to take a drink at the bar rather than at a table.

Mealtimes

The locals eat just a little earlier on the islands than do people on the mainland. Breakfast may start at about 7:30 A.M. and go on until 10:00 P.M. Lunch runs typically from 1:00 to 3:00 P.M. and dinner usually begins at around 8:30 P.M., although some people may be drifting in to eat as late as 10:30 P.M.

The aromatic local liqueur is worth sampling—you may even grow to like it.

In most hotels concessions have been made to impatient tourists, however, and they may start serving breakfast at 7:00 A.M., with lunch at 12:30 P.M. and dinner served as outrageously early as 7:00 P.M.

Breakfast

The Spanish make a point of treating breakfast as unimportant. The islanders are no great exception, despite having their own delicious *ensaimada*—a floatingly light round bun, presented as a spiral of dough sprinkled with icing sugar. If eaten with cream, almonds, or pumpkin jam, it makes a sinful snack at any time, but it is delightful for breakast, served with coffee on a sunny terrace. Go ahead, dunk it—you may start a habit you'll find hard to kick. At Palma airport, you'll see addicts taking home special flat boxes nearly a yard across containing *ensaimadas*.

Hotels seem to write their own rules when it comes to breakfasts, which range from vast buffets included in the room rate to a bread roll and tasteless coffee for which you have to pay extra. If the latter's the case, head out to a bar or cafeteria, where you will be sure of great coffee. Some of them offer an "English breakfast" of bacon and eggs, too.

Drinks

There's no question about it, the islands truly are a drinker's paradise. Wonderful fresh fruit juices abound. Try some of the unusual thirst-quenching mixtures such as peach-and-grape. The local beer is fairly cheap, good, and served cold, but if you want the one you always have in the pub at home, it's probably here too. In the bigger resorts, there is a staggering (the word being extremely appropriate at times) selection of British, German, and Dutch beers, as well as other draught and bottled brands at about twice the domestic price.

Mallorca produces its own wines in various lowland areas and sheltered spots, particularly around Binissalem, and it's interesting to try them—they may not be very distinguished

Tasty Tapas

The days are sadly gone when you were given a free bite of food with your drink in a bar, but the word for these morsels survives. *Tapa* means "lid," from the little plate that covered the glass and carried the snack. Some bars specialize in *tapas*, featuring a line of dishes, hot and cold, for you to pick from. Portions are larger now that you're paying for them: perhaps five different choices is enough to substitute for a conventional main course.

You don't need to know the tapa names, you can just point. It's a great way of making new discoveries among a range that might run from meat balls to potato salad, tripe, eels, or stewed baby octopuses. Look out for *boquerones*, anchovies freshly prepared, not tinned, in vinegar, oil, and garlic, and, most common of all on *tapa* counters, the *tortilla* of eggs, potatoes, and onions, fried until golden in olive oil.

(the firm Jaume Mesquida is considered by some to produce the best) though they're better than the inferior bulk wines that some restaurants serve up as house wines. Ordering the house wine (*vino de la casa*) is a useful economy measure—and many Spanish diners do it without a second thought—but some of it is dreadful. Ask what it is, and whether you can have a taste. If you want something better, try some of the much-improved Catalan wines (Penedés produces the best) or the Riojas, white or red.

Spanish sparkling wines can be cheap and mass-produced. The word *cava* tends to be applied indiscriminately, though theoretically it should be reserved for the better bubbly produced by the same method as champagne. Some of these wines might be sweeter than you're used to; if you really want it dry, look for *brut* (even *seco*, "dry," may not be such).

Sangría is a favourite summer wine and fruit mixture—every bar has its own recipe. Beware, it's often so cool and smooth that you don't realize the kick it can have.

To many, Spain means sherry (*jerez*), and there is every kind here. The pale, dry *fino* is sometimes drunk not only as an apéritif but with soup and fish courses. Rich dark *oloroso* goes well after dinner. Spanish brandy varies from excellent to rough: you usually get what you pay for. Gin has been produced in Menorca since the British Navy was there, and several brands come from the mainland, too. Other spirits are made under licence in Spain, and are usually a lot cheaper than imported Scotch whisky, for example. There are "lookalikes" as well, which imitate the labels of some well-known brands. Hitting below the belt, some bars may refill famousname bottles with something that ought to be a lot cheaper.

Finally, to round off a meal, try one of the locally made liqueurs, either aromatic *hierbas seca* ("dry herbs"), *hierbas dulce* ("sweet herbs") or sticky *palo*, made from carob seeds.

INDEX

HANDY TRAVEL TIPS

An A–Z Summary of Practical Information

A

ACCOMMODATION

(See also CAMPING *on page 105 and the list of* RECOMMENDED HOTELS starting on page 129)

Prices are not government-controlled but they must be posted at reception desks and in rooms. Off-season, you may be able to negotiate lower rates, but note that most resort hotels close for the winter, reducing your choice. In the height of summer, they may be filled by the clients of package tour operators who have reserved the accommodation in advance.

Accommodation ranges across a broad spectrum. You can find a room in a *pensión* (boarding house), *hostal* (modest hotel), resort hotel with sports and entertainment facilities, or *de luxe* palace in city or countryside. Breakfast may be included in the room rate; check before booking. On arrival, a guest normally signs a registration card which should also state the hotel category, room number, and room rate. In practice, reception clerks often fill in the details later with the aid of the guest's passport.

Hotels are officially graded by stars, one to five, according to their facilities. *Hostales* are graded from one to three stars. The grading is posted at the front door. But grades are not always a reflection of quality: some one-star places can be superior to others with three.

Increasingly popular in the Mediterranean are package arrangements including accommodation in furnished apartments or villas. These are usually part of a complex with amenities, such as a swimming pool, gardens, or sports facilities, depending on the price. Tour companies' brochures should give a full and accurate description.

I'd like a double/single room.	**Quisiera una habitación doble/sencilla.**
with/without bath/shower	**con/sin baño/ducha**
What's the rate per night?	**¿Cuál es el precio por noche?**

AIRPORTS *(aeropuerto)*

Mallorca. Son Sant Joan Airport, Palma de Mallorca (PMI), has two terminals: Terminal A for scheduled flights and some charters, Terminal B for charter flights only. Free luggage trolleys are available. A tourist information office, hotel-reservation, car-hire and currency-exchange counters, post office, restaurant, bar, souvenir and duty-free shops (international departures only) are at your disposal. Taxis and regular buses link the airport with Palma, a 15-minute trip. Official taxi fares to all parts of the island are posted by the airport exit doors. The bus service operates to Plaça de Espanya (the terminal is near Palma's two railway stations) every half-hour from early morning to midnight. Tour-company representatives and hotel coaches meet charter-flight passengers.

Menorca. Mahón (Maó) Airport (MAH) is only 5 km (3 miles), a few minutes' taxi ride, from the city. There are no regular buses. The airport's international traffic operates only from May to October, and many of its facilities (tourist information, duty-free shop) open only during that period. Car-hire desks, café, and bar operate year-round.

B

BICYCLE and MOTORSCOOTER HIRE *(bicicletas/escúteres de alquiler)*

A practical and enjoyable way to see the islands is to hire a bicycle by the hour or day. Mopeds and motorscooters are also available in most resorts, but you'll need a licence exclusively for them. Prices vary widely, so shop around. Remember that wearing crash-helmets is compulsory when riding a motorcycle, whatever the engine capacity, though you'd never guess it from seeing the locals.

I'd like to hire a bicycle.	**Quisiera alquilar una bicicleta.**
What's the charge per day/week?	**¿Cuánto cobran por día/semana?**

C

CAMPING (*camping*)

Pitching your tent just where the fancy takes you is most definitely frowned upon by the island authorities, and you'll be asked unceremoniously to move on. You may be able to camp on private land, but be sure to ask permission of the owner first.

There are two official camping sites on **Mallorca**, both at the north end of the island:

Camping Club San Pedro, Artá, tel. 58 90 23, open April to September. Situated near the beach with its own swimming pool, hot and cold showers, bar/restaurant, and supermarket.

Camping Platja Blava, Muro, tel. 53 78 63, open all year. The site is within walking distance of the beach and has many facilities, including swimming pools, tennis courts, showers and baths, bars/restaurant, supermarket, and disco.

Menorca has one official camping site 3 km (2 miles) from Cala Galdana:

Camping S'Atalaia, Ferreríes, tel. 37 30 95, open May to September. Situated amidst pine woods 4 km (2½ miles) from Ferreríes. Facilities include swimming pool, showers, restaurant/bar, and supermarket.

For all the campsites listed above, you are advised to book ahead during the peak season in July and August.

May we camp here?	**¿Podemos acampar aquí?**
We have a tent.	**Tenemos una tienda de camping.**

CAR HIRE (*coches de alquiler*) (See also DRIVING on page 111)

There are car-hire firms in most resorts, main towns and at the airports. Ask for special seasonal rates and discounts and find out what insurance cover is included. A value-added tax (IVA) of 15% is added to the total charge, but will have been included if you have pre-paid the car hire before arrival (normally the way to obtain the lowest rates). Third-party insurance is included, but full collision

coverage is advisable as well. Unlimited free mileage is always included in the Balearics. General conditions may include a refundable
deposit, but holders of major credit cards are usually exempt.

You should be over 21, and have had your full licence at least 6
months. You should also have an International Driving Permit, but
the hire companies in practice accept your ordinary national licence.
So, probably, will the police if you are stopped by them, though they
might insist on an official Spanish translation.

Most sizes of car are available, including 4-wheel drives and con-
vertibles, but the vast majority are small economy models. They're
well suited to the narrow rural roads and mountain hairpin bends.

I'd like to rent a car (tomorrow).	**Quisiera alquilar un coche (para mañana).**
for one day/a week	**por un día/una semana**
Please include full insurance cover.	**Haga el favor de incluir el seguro a todo riesgo.**

CLIMATE and CLOTHING

Sun-seekers hit the beaches from May to October and the sea is
pleasantly warm for swimming from June or July to October. July
and August can be oven-hot as well as very crowded. Mallorca en-
joys a mild winter, too, making a tempting break for visitors from
northern Europe. It can be chilly and wet at times, of course, but a
wall of mountains along the northwest coast protects the rest of the
island from the worst of the winter weather. The tourist season has
been getting longer: March and April bring a rush of cyclists, soon
followed by walkers and bird-watchers.

Menorca can be swept by cold winds in winter and early spring.
The holiday season there runs from early May to the end of October,
with few hotels open the rest of the year.

These average temperatures and sunshine figures apply to Palma.

	J	F	M	A	M	J	J	A	S	O	N	D
Max °F	57	59	62	66	71	79	84	84	80	73	64	59
Max °C	14	15	17	19	22	26	29	29	27	23	18	15

Mallorca and Menorca

	J	F	M	A	M	J	J	A	S	O	N	D
Min °F	43	43	46	50	55	62	68	68	64	57	50	46
Min °C	6	6	8	10	13	17	20	20	18	14	10	8
Days of sunshine	15	14	16	19	20	22	28	26	20	16	14	14

Clothing. From June to September the days are always hot — wear lightweight cotton clothes — but take along a jacket or sweater for the evening. Remember also to take a long-sleeved shirt or sunhat to protect against the strong midday sun. During the rest of the year a light jacket and a raincoat or umbrella will come in handy.

Although the prevailing attitude is towards casual dress, some hotels, restaurants and nightclubs object to men wearing shorts and tee-shirts, and a shirt and tie at least are expected at dinner. Respectable clothing should, of course, be worn when visiting churches.

Walking shoes and/or boots are advisable if you are planning island walking during your stay. Take a small backpack to carry lightweight waterproofs and refreshment if you intend to tackle the hills.

COMMUNICATIONS (See also TIME DIFFERENCES on page 124)

Post offices (*correos*) are for mail and telegrams: you can't usually telephone from them. Opening hours are usually 9am-2pm Monday to Friday, 9am-1pm Saturday. The main post office in Palma is open daily 9am-9pm; the main post office in Mahón is open for stamps 4-6pm Monday to Friday.

Stamps (*sello*) can also be bought at the official Tabac and at some shops selling postcards and cigarettes. Mailboxes are bright yellow.

If you don't know in advance where you'll be staying, you can have your mail addressed to the *Lista de Correos* (poste restante or general delivery) in the nearest town. Take your passport to the post office as identification when you want to collect any letters. There may be a small charge.

Telegrams (*telegrama*) and **fax**. The main telegraph offices are at the main post offices: in Palma at Constitució 6, tel. 72 10 95; in Mahón at Bonaire 15, tel. 36 38 92. Telegrams are expensive, and remember that there is no telegram delivery in the U.K. It will usually be quicker, cheaper and more convenient to fax. Most hotels with fax facilities are happy to allow guests to send and receive faxes, but this service is liable to a supplementary charge. Fax machines for public use can be found in communication centres in most holiday resorts.

Telephone (*teléfono*). The telephone office is independent of the post office and is identified by a blue and white sign. You can make direct-dial local and international calls from public telephone booths in the street. Most operate both with coins and cards; international telephone credit cards can also be used. Instructions for use are given in several languages in the booths, which are widely distributed throughout the islands. Calls can also be made from hotels, usually with a surcharge.

For international calls, have a supply of coins (25, 50, or 100 ptas.; don't use 5 ptas. coins which may break the connection). Pick up the receiver, wait for the dialling tone, dial 07, wait for a further tone and then dial the country code, area code (without initial 0) and number. The coins will drop in as needed from the slot provided.

Dial the operator (9398) if you wish to make a person-to-person (*persona a persona*) call or to reverse the charges/make a collect call (*cobro revertido*), for which you have to make a 700 ptas. deposit — refunded if the call is accepted.

Telephone cards can be purchased from the official Tabac in units of 1,000 and 2,000 ptas.

Can you get me this number in...?	**¿Puede comunicarme con este número en...?**
Have you received any mail for...?	**¿Ha recibido correo para...?**
A stamp for this letter/postcard please.	**Por favor, un sello para esta carta/tarjeta postal.**
express (special delivery)	**urgente**
airmail	**vía aérea**
registered	**certificado**
I would like to send a telegram to...	**Quisiera mandar un telegrama a...**

Mallorca and Menorca

COMPLAINTS

By law, all hotels, restaurants, and campsites must have official complaint forms (*Hoja Oficial de Reclamación/Full Oficial de Reclamació*) and produce them on demand. The original of this document should be sent to the regional office of the Ministry of Tourism, one copy remains with the establishment complained against ,and you keep the third sheet. Merely asking for a complaint form is often enough to resolve most matters since tourism authorities take a serious view of complaints and your hosts want to keep their licence.

Legislation has been introduced that greatly strengthens the consumer's hand — inspections are being carried out and inaccurate information made punishable by law. You might be referred to the consumer protection office (Dirección General de Consumo, via Roma 18, Palma). For a tourist's needs, however, the tourist office, or in really serious cases, the police, would be able to handle the situation or at least advise where to go. In Palma, the police can call upon interpreters in the main foreign languages spoken by visitors.

CRIME

Spain's crime rate has caught up with that of other European countries and the Balearics have not been immune. Be on your guard against purse-snatchers and pickpockets (sometimes posing as carnation sellers near Palma cathedral), especially in busy places, markets, fiestas, sports events, and Palma streets (particularly the area of Plaça Major, which should be given a wide berth at night).

The rules are the ones you might follow almost anywhere. Don't leave valuables unattended or take them to the beach. Make use of hotel safe-boxes. Don't carry large sums of money or expensive jewellery. Lock cars and never leave cases, bags, cameras, etc., on view.

In Palma or Manacor, report thefts and break-ins to the Policía Nacional, elsewhere to the Guardia Civil.

I want to report a theft.	**Quiero denunciar un robo.**
My handbag/ticket/wallet/	**Me han robado el**
passport has been stolen.	**bolso/el billete/la**
	cartera/el pasaporte.

CUSTOMS *(aduana)* **and ENTRY FORMALITIES** (See also
EMBASSIES AND CONSULATES on page 115)

Most visitors require only a valid passport to enter Spain. U.K. citizens should note that the British Visitor's Passport is no longer accepted for entry to Spain. Visitors from South Africa must have visas, and those from Australia may only stay for one month and make no more than two entries in that time, unless they have a visa. New Zealanders are permitted one month's stay and only one entry per year without a visa. Most visitors are allowed to stay for 90 days (U.S. citizens 180 days). Full information on passport and visa regulations is available from the Spanish Embassy in your country.

As Spain is part of the European Union (EU), free exchange of non-duty-free items for personal use is permitted between **Spain** and the **UK** and the **Republic of Ireland**. However, duty-free items are still subject to restrictions. Residents of non-EU countries can take home the following amounts:

Into:	Cigarettes	Cigars	Tobacco	Spirits	Wine	Beer
Australia	250	or	250g	1*l*	or	1*l*	
Canada	200	and 50	400g	1.1*l*	or 1.1*l*	or 8.5*l*
New Zealand	200	or 50	or 250g	1.1*l*	4.5*l*	or 4.5*l*
South Africa	400	and 50	and 250g	1*l*	2*l*	
U.S.A.	200	and 100	a reasonable amount	1*l*	or	1*l*	

Currency restrictions. There are no limits on the amount of money, Spanish or foreign, that you may import. Departing, you should declare sums over the equivalent of 500,000 ptas. It is wise, therefore, to declare such amounts on entry if you plan to take them out again.

D

DRIVING

To take your car into Spain, you should have:

● your driving licence, and an International Driving Permit (not obligatory for most EU citizens — ask your automobile association

— but recommended in case of difficulties as it has a text in Spanish) or a legalized and certified translation of your driving licence
- car registration papers
- Green Card (an extension to your regular insurance policy, making it valid for foreign countries)
- nationality sticker on the back of the vehicle.

Also strongly recommended: A bail bond, obtainable from your insurance company or automobile association. If you were to injure somebody in Spain, you could be imprisoned while the accident is under investigation. This bond will bail you out.

When driving, be sure to carry all the required papers (or photocopies), including car hire documents.

Driving conditions on Mallorca and Menorca. The rules are the same as in Spain: drive on the right, overtake (pass) on the left, yield right of way to vehicles coming from the right (unless your road is marked as having priority). Front and rear seat belts are compulsory.

Main roads are well-surfaced and Mallorca has a few stretches of motorway. Secondary roads on Mallorca are narrow but good; on Menorca they can be very narrow, rough and unsignposted. Minor roads no better than stony tracks abound, especially on Menorca.

Traffic police. The roads are patrolled by the Traffic Civil Guard (*Guardia Civil de Tráfico*) on motorcycles. Courteous and helpful, they are also tough on lawbreakers. Fines are payable on the spot.

You might be stopped for: speeding; travelling too close to the car in front; overtaking (passing) without using your direction indicators; travelling at night with a burned-out light (Spanish law requires you to carry a full set of spare bulbs at all times); or failing to come to a complete halt at a stop sign.

Speed limits are 120 km/h (75 mph) on motorways, 100 km/h (62 mph) on broad main roads (two lanes each way), 90 km/h (56mph) on other main roads, 50 km/h (31 mph), or as marked, in densely populated areas.

Beware of drinking and driving. The permitted blood-alcohol level is low and fines for exceeding the limit are intended to deter.

Parking can be difficult in towns. Foreign and mainland-registered vehicles are not immune from wheel-clamping and towing away if they park illegally or overstay time limits.

Fuel and oil. Service stations are plentiful on Mallorca but not Menorca. Petrol (gasoline) comes in 95 (Euro super lead-free), 97 (super) and 98 (lead-free super plus) grades, but not all at every station. Diesel fuel is widely available.

Fluid measures

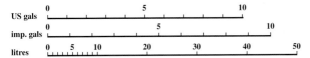

Distance

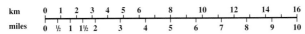

Breakdowns. Balearic garages are as efficient as any, and the mechanics can be ingenious, but repairs may take time in busy tourist areas. Spare parts are readily available for Spanish-built cars and many other popular models. For less common makes, they may have to be imported. Kits of basic spare parts are obtainable from some automobile associations (refund available upon return home, if kit not used).

Road signs. Most signs are the standard pictographs used throughout Europe. However, you may encounter the following written signs (see page 114), in Spanish or amended into *Mallorquí* or *Menorquí*.

Mallorca and Menorca

¡Alto!	Stop!
Aparcamiento	Parking
Autopista	Motorway
Calzada deteriorada	Bad road
Calzada estrecha	Narrow road
Ceda el paso	Give way (yield)
Cruce peligroso	Dangerous crossroads
Curva peligrosa	Dangerous bend
Despacio	Slow
Peligro	Danger
Prohibido adelantar	No overtaking (passing)
Prohibido aparcar	No parking
(International) Driving Permit	**Carné de conducir (internacional)**
Car registration papers	**Permiso de circulación**
Green Card	**Carta verde**
Are we on the right road for...?	**¿Es ésta la carretera hacia...?**
Full tank, please. lead-free	**Lléno el depósito, por favor. sin plomo**
Can I park here?	**¿Puedo aparcar aquí?**
My car has broken down.	**Mi coche se ha estropeado.**
There's been an accident.	**Ha habido un accidente.**

E

ELECTRIC CURRENT *(corriente eléctrica)*

220 volts is almost standard, but older installations of 125 volts, although becoming rare in tourist facilities, may still be found, sometimes alongside the 220-volt system. Check before plugging in. If the voltage is 125, American appliances will operate. If it is 220, you will need a transformer to operate them.

What's the voltage?	**¿Cuál es el voltaje?**
an adaptor/a battery	**un adaptador/una pila**

EMBASSIES and CONSULATES *(embajada; consulado)*

Canada: For minor matters contact the British consulate, Palma (or Honorary Vice-Consul, Menorca). Other cases: Consulate General, Edif. Goya, Calle Núñez de Balboa 35, 28001 Madrid; tel. 431 43 00

Eire (Honorary Consul): Sant Miquel 68 (8th floor), Palma; tel. 71 92 44

U.K. (also for Commonwealth citizens): Plaça Major 3-D, Palma; tel. 71 24 45

(Honorary Vice-Consul, Menorca): Carrer Torret 28, Sant Lluis; tel. 36 64 39

U.S.A. (consular agency): Avda del Rei Jaume III 26, Palma; tel. 72 26 60

Where's the British/American consulate?	**¿Dónde está el consulado británico/americano?**

EMERGENCIES *(See also* EMBASSIES AND CONSULATES *on page 115,* MEDICAL CARE *on page 118, and* POLICE *on page 122)*

If you are not staying in a hotel, telephone or visit the local Municipal Police or the Guardia Civil. Try to take a Spanish speaker with you. Here are a few important telephone numbers (check the front of the phone book for other numbers):

Mallorca		**Menorca**	
Police		091	091
First aid *(casas de socorro)* (Mahón)		72 21 79 (Palma)	36 12 21
Fire brigade *(bomberos)* (Mahón)		080 (Palma)	36 39 61

Police!	**¡Policía!**	Help!	**¡Socorro!**
Fire!	**¡Fuego!**	Stop!	**¡Deténgase!**

Mallorca and Menorca

ETIQUETTE

The islanders are open and hospitable, easy to talk to and generous. Politeness and simple courtesies still matter. A handshake on greeting and leaving is normal. Always begin any conversation, whether with a friend, shop assistant, taxi-driver or telephone operator, with a *buenos días* (good morning) or *buenas tardes* (good afternoon). *¡Hola!* (Hello!) is a frequent island substitute. Always say *adiós* (goodbye) or *buenas noches* (good night) when leaving. *Por favor* (please) should begin all requests.

How are you?	¿Cómo está usted?
Do you speak English?	¿Habla usted inglés?
I don't speak Spanish.	No hablo español.

GUIDES and TOURS

For an English-speaking guide on Mallorca, apply to the Grupo Sindical de Informadores Turísticos, Miquel Marqués 13, Palma (near the railway and bus terminals); tel. 46 09 30.

On Menorca, a list is available at the Tourist Information Office, Plaça Esplanada 40, Mahón); tel. 36 37 90.

| We'd like an English-speaking guide. | Queremos un guía que hable inglés. |
| I need an English interpreter. | Necesito un intérprete de inglés. |

LANGUAGE

The islands are bilingual (at least). The national language, Castilian Spanish, is understood everywhere. In addition, *Mallorquí* is spoken in Mallorca and *Menorquí* in Menorca. These are dialects of Catalan.

Many islanders speak Castilian with a marked but clear accent, but English is widely understood in resort areas and by people used to dealing with visitors. So to a lesser extent are German and French.

Mallorquí/Menorquí	**Castilian**	
Welcome	*Benvinguts*	*Bienvenido*
Good morning	*Bon dia*	*Buenos días*
Good afternoon/evening	*Bona tarda*	*Buenas tardes*
Good night	*Bon nit*	*Buenas noches*
Please	*Si us plau*	*Por favor*
Thank you	*Graciès*	*Gracias*
Goodbye	*Adéu*	*Adiós*

Everywhere you'll hear an all-purpose expression, *es igual* ("it's the same," meaning anything from "you're welcome" to "who cares?."

The Berlitz SPANISH PHRASE BOOK AND DICTIONARY covers most situations you're likely to encounter in your travels through the islands. And the Berlitz Spanish-English/English-Spanish pocket dictionary contains a 12,500-word glossary of each language, plus a menu-reader supplement.

LAUNDRY and DRY-CLEANING *(lavandería; tintorería)*

Most hotels will handle laundry and dry-cleaning but they'll usually charge more than an independent establishment. Major resorts have self-service launderettes and the best-equipped villas and apartments have washing machines.

Where's the nearest laundry/dry-cleaners?	**¿Dónde está la lavandería/ tintorería más cercana?**

LOST PROPERTY

The first thing to do when you discover you've lost something is, obviously, to retrace your steps. If nothing comes to light, report the loss to the Municipal Police or Guardia Civil. You will need a copy of the report if you are going to make a claim on an insurance policy.

I've lost my wallet/handbag/ passport.	**He perdido mi cartera/bolso/pasaporte.**

M

MEDIA

Newspapers and magazines (*periódico*; *revista*). In main tourist areas most European, including British, newspapers are sold on the day of publication. So are the Paris-based *International Herald Tribune* and European edition of *The Wall Street Journal*. Principal European and American magazines are available.

The *Mallorca — Daily Bulletin* ("Daily Bee") is a newspaper published six days a week in Palma for English-speaking residents and visitors. On Menorca, you can find a monthly English-language paper called *Roqueta*.

Radio and television (*radio*; *televisión*). A short-wave set will pick up all European capitals. Reception of Britain's BBC World Service is usually good to excellent. A good set will receive the BBC long-wave and even medium-wave domestic programmes. The local radio station in Palma broadcasts in English 24 hours a day on 103.2 FM.

Most hotels and bars have television, usually tuned to sports (international or local), and broadcasting in Castilian, Catalan (from Barcelona), and *Mallorquí*. Satellite dishes are sprouting, and feeding multiple channels (German, French, Sky, BBC, CNN, Super, etc.) to many hotels and private homes.

Have you any English-language newspapers/magazines? **¿Tienen periódicos/revistas en inglés?**

MEDICAL CARE

Standards of hygiene are generally high, and any intestinal disorder of travellers is more likely to be due to an excess of sun or alcohol.

Although there are rarely more than a few mosquitoes, just one can ruin a night's sleep. Bring your own anti-mosquito devices, or buy them locally — or you can often use a spray available at the hotel reception desk.

It is well worth taking out insurance to cover the risk of illness or accident when on holiday. This is normally available as part of a general travel insurance package.

There are doctors in all towns and their consulting hours are displayed. For less serious matters, first-aid personnel, called *practicantes*, make daily rounds of the larger resort hotels, and some hotels have a nurse on duty. In case of need, enquire at your hotel, or, away from hotels, ask the police or tourist offices for help.

Pharmacies (*farmacia*) are open during normal shopping hours but there is at least one per town open all night, the *farmacia de guardia*. Its location is posted in the windows of all other pharmacies. Spanish pharmacists are highly trained and respected, and for minor problems you can consult them before or instead of going to a doctor.

Hospitals

Mallorca: Hospital Son Dureta, Andrea Doria 55, Palma, tel. 17 50 00; Policlinic Miramar, Camino Vecinal La Vileta, tel. 45 02 12.

Menorca: Hospital Municipal, Cos de Gracia 26, Mahón, tel. 36 12 21.

U.K. citizens with EU form E111 obtained well before departure can receive free emergency treatment at Social Security and Municipal hospitals in Spain.

Where's the nearest (all-night) pharmacy?	**¿Dónde está la farmacia (de guardia) más cercana?**
I need a doctor/dentist.	**Necesito un médico/dentista.**
a fever/sunburn	**fiebre/quemadura del sol**
an upset stomach	**molestias de estómago**

MONEY MATTERS *(See also* Customs and Entry Formalities *on page 111)*

Currency (*moneda*). The monetary unit of Spain is the *peseta* (abbreviated *pta.*).

 Coins: 1, 5, 10, 25, 50, 100, 200, 500 ptas.
 Banknotes: 1,000, 2,000, 5,000, 10,000 ptas.
 A 5-peseta coin is traditionally called a *duro*.

Credit cards. The major international cards are widely recognized, though smaller businesses tend to prefer cash. Cards linked to Visa/Eurocard/MasterCard are most generally accepted. They are also useful for obtaining cash advances from banks.

Eurocheques. You'll have no problem settling bills with Eurocheques, provided you have the Eurocheque encashment card.

Exchange offices. Many travel agencies and other businesses displaying a *cambio* sign will change foreign currency into ptas., and stay open outside banking hours. The rate is likely to be a bit less favourable than at the banks. Both banks and exchange offices pay slightly more for traveller's cheques than for cash. Always take your passport when you go to change money.

Traveller's cheques. Hotels, shops, restaurants, and travel agencies cash them, and so do banks, where you're likely to get a better rate (you will need your passport). Try to cash small amounts at a time, keeping some of your holiday funds in cheques, in the hotel safe.

Where's the nearest bank/currency exchange office?	**¿Dónde está el banco/la oficina de cambio más cercana?**
I want to change some pounds/dollars.	**Quiero cambiar libras/dólares.**
Do you accept traveller's cheques?	**¿Aceptan cheques de viaje?**
Can I pay with this credit card?	**¿Puedo pagar con esta tarjeta de crédito?**
How much is that?	**¿Cuánto es?**

PLANNING YOUR BUDGET

To give you an idea of what to expect, here are some average prices in Spanish ptas. However, they must be regarded as approximate, as inflation pushes costs relentlessly higher. Rates of exchange fluctuate, so check the latest figures for your currency.

Prices quoted may be subject to a VAT/sales tax (IVA) of either 6%, 15%, or 28%.

Airport transfer. *Mallorca*: bus to Palma 230 ptas, taxi from 2,000 ptas. *Menorca*: no airport bus, taxi to Mahón centre about 1,300 ptas.

Babysitters. 800-1,400 ptas./hour.

Bicycle and motorscooter hire. Bicycle per day 750 ptas., moped per day 2,000 ptas., scooter per day about 2,900 ptas.

Car hire (unlimited mileage, insurance included). *Seat Marbella* 3,100 ptas./day, 20,000 ptas./week; *Ford Escort* 5,560 ptas./day, 35,000 ptas./week. Add 15% tax. (Note: rates are highly seasonal, and can be much lower if car hire is paid for in advance through travel agents/companies.)

Entertainment. Bullfight 1,800 ptas. and up, cinema 500 ptas. and up, nightclub/flamenco/cabaret show from 3,000 ptas., disco (admission and first drink) ,about 1,000 ptas. (some free entry).

Hairdressers. *Woman's* haircut 2,500 ptas., shampoo and set or blow-dry 2,000 ptas.; *man's* haircut 1,500 ptas.

Hotels (double room with bath). ***** 20,700-49,000 ptas., **** 8,000-25,000 ptas., *** 3,500-16,000 ptas., ** 2,600-9,000 ptas., * 2,000-7,000 ptas.

Meals and drinks. Continental breakfast 250-400 ptas., *plato del día* from 750 ptas., *menú del día* from 850 ptas., lunch/dinner in good restaurant 3,500 ptas. and up, beer (small bottle or glass) 175-250 ptas., coffee 135-150 ptas., Spanish brandy 275 ptas., soft drinks from 150 ptas., bottle of house wine 650 ptas., other wines from 1,000 ptas.

Shopping bag. Loaf of bread 80-280 ptas., 250g of butter 275 ptas., 6 eggs 150 ptas., beefsteak (500g) 800 ptas., 250g of coffee 250 ptas., 100g of instant coffee 390 ptas., mineral water 95 ptas., fruit juice (1 litre) 175 ptas., bottle of wine 175 ptas. and up.

Sports. *Golf* green fees 5,500-7,000 ptas. per day, *tennis* court fee 1,000 ptas./hour, *horseback-riding* from 1,500 ptas./hour, *water-skiing* about 2,000 ptas. per tow, 4,000 ptas./hour with lesson, *windsurfer* hire about 1,800 ptas./hour (negotiate day rates).

OPENING HOURS

Schedules revolve around the siesta, and most **shops** and **offices** therefore open from 9am to 1 or 2pm and again from 4 or 5pm until 8pm or later. Big **supermarkets** may stay open throughout the day.

Post offices are usually Monday to Friday 9am-2pm, Saturday 9am-1pm. **Banks** generally open Monday-Friday 8:30/9am-2:30pm (1:30pm in summer), Saturdays 9am-1pm (except summer). Hours vary from town to town. Some banks stay open until 4:30pm (Monday-Thursday, mid-September to mid-June).

Restaurants serve lunch from 1 to 3:30pm. In the evenings their timing depends on the kind of customers they expect. Locals probably want to eat between 8:30 and 11pm (rather earlier than on the mainland); places catering for foreigners may function from 7pm.

PHOTOGRAPHY

Major brands of film are available, but you should always check the expiration date before purchasing. Bear in mind that all photographic equipment and supplies tend to be expensive in Mallorca and Menorca, so it's advisable to bring an adequate supply of film and spare batteries with you. Several express photo shops can develop your prints in one hour, though processing is expensive. For handy tips on how to get the most out of your holiday photographs, refer to the Berlitz-Nikon Pocket Guide to Travel Photography.

POLICE *(policía)*

There are three police forces in Spain: the *Policía Municipal*, who are attached to the local town hall, the *Cuerpo Nacional de Policía*, a national anti-crime unit, and the *Guardia Civil*, the national police force patrolling town and country, including the roads.

If you need police assistance, you can call on any one of the three. Spanish police are efficient, strict, and courteous to foreign visitors.

Where's the nearest police station? **¿Dónde está la comisaría más cercana?**

PUBLIC HOLIDAYS *(fiesta)*

1 January	*Año Nuevo*	New Year's Day
6 January	*Epifanía*	Epiphany
20 January	*San Sebastián*	St. Sebastian's Day
1 May	*Día del Trabajo*	Labour Day
25 July	*Santiago Apóstol*	St. James's Day
15 August	*Asunción*	Assumption
12 October	*Día de la Hispanidad*	Discovery of America Day (Columbus Day)
1 November	*Todos los Santos*	All Saints' Day
6 December	*Día de la Española*	Constitution Day
25 December	*Navidad Constitución*	Christmas Day
26 December	*La Fiesta Navidad*	Christmas Holiday
Movable dates:	*Jueves Santo*	Maundy Thursday
	Viernes Santo	Good Friday
	Lunes de Pascua	Easter Monday (Balearics)
	Corpus Christi	Corpus Christi
	Inmaculada Concepción	Immaculate Conception
	(normally 8 December)	

R

RELIGION

The national religion of Spain is Roman Catholicism. Enquire at the tourist office for information on services in foreign languages.

123

T

TIME DIFFERENCES

The Balearics keep the same time as mainland Spain. Clocks go forward one hour in spring and back one hour in autumn. The chart below shows the difference between Spain and some selected cities.

Los Angeles	Chicago	New York	London	**Mallorca**
3am	5am	6am	11am	**noon**

What time is it?   **¿Qué hora es?**

TIPPING

Since a service charge is normally included in hotel and restaurant bills, tipping is not obligatory. However, it's normal to leave a small coin (up to 5% of the bill) after service at a bar counter, and 5-10% on restaurant bills. Further rough guidelines:

Hotel porter, per bag	50–100 ptas.
Lavatory attendant	25-50 ptas.
Waiter	10% (optional)
Taxi driver	10% (optional)
Tourist guide	10%

TOILETS

There are many expressions for "toilets" in Spanish: *aseos, servicios, WC, water,* and *retretes.* The first two are the more common. Toilet doors have a "C" for *Caballeros* (gentlemen), an "S" for *Señoras* (ladies), or a pictograph. Public toilets exist in some large towns, but almost every bar and restaurant has one available for public use. It's polite to buy a coffee or drink if you drop in to use the conveniences.

Where are the toilets?   **¿Dónde están los servicios?**

TOURIST INFORMATION OFFICES *(oficina de turismo)*

Spanish National Tourist Offices are maintained in many countries:

Australia: International House, Suite 44, 104 Bathurst St, P.O. Box A-675, 2000 Sydney NSW; tel. (02) 264 79 66

Canada: 62 Bloor St. West, Suite 201, Toronto, Ontario M4W 3E2; tel. (416) 961-31 31

U.K.:   57-58 St. James's St, London SW1A 1LD; tel. (171) 499-0901

U.S.A.:   Water Tower Place, Suite 915 East, 845 North Michigan Ave, Chicago, IL 60611; tel. (312) 944-0216/642-1992

8383 Wilshire Blvd, Suite 960, 90211 Beverly Hills, CA 90211; tel. (213) 658-7188

666 5th Ave, New York, NY 10103; tel. (212) 265-8822

1221 Brickell Ave., Miami, FL 33131; tel. (305) 358-1992

Major resorts on Mallorca have their own tourist information offices:

Palma: Oficina de Información Turística, Avinguda del Rei Jaume III 10; tel. 71 22 16. Fomento de Turismo, Carrer de Constitució 1; tel. 72 53 96. Oficina de Información Turística, Palma Airport; tel. 26 08 03.

Menorca: Oficina de Información Turística, Plaça Esplanada, Mahón; tel. 36 37 90.

Where is the tourist office?   **¿Dónde está laoficina de turismo?**

TRANSPORT

Mallorca has a reliable and comprehensive public transport system serving almost all towns and villages. Collect an up-to-date bus and train (FEVE) timetable from the tourist information office, as well as a local bus timetable from the nearest bus station (*estación de autobuses*). Note that that public services finish early, at around 8:45pm.

Mallorca and Menorca

Buses. Mallorca is well served by bus lines, and its buses are economical, clean, and easy to use. The drivers are friendly and helpful. Destinations are marked on the front of the bus, and each town has its own main bus stop or terminal. In Palma, most services start from Plaça de Espanya, Plaça Sant Antoní, or Plaça de la Reina.

Menorca's bus system is much more limited, but services run between the main towns. In Mahón most start from Plaça Esplanada or nearby Avinguda J M Quadrado.

For information, ask at a bus station or tourist information office.

Taxis. Taxis in Spain compare very favourably with those in other countries. Check the fare before you get in: rates are fixed and are displayed in several languages in the taxi. If you take a long trip you may be charged a two-way fare whether you return or not.

Trains (*tren*). Mallorca has two narrow-gauge lines, starting from neighbouring stations on Plaça de Espanya, Palma. One goes to Inca, but the more picturesque line links Palma and Sóller, and makes five runs in each direction every day (six on Sundays). (See page 39).

When's the next bus/train to...?	**¿Cuándo sale el próximo autobús/tren para...?**
A ticket to...	**Un billete para...**
single (one-way)	**ida**
return (round-trip)	**ida y vuelta**
What's the fare to...?	**¿Cuánto es la tarifa a ...?**

TRAVELLERS with DISABILITIES

A number of hotels are suitable for travellers with disabilities, though it is advisable to check before making a reservation. Hotels near the beaches in the bigger resorts are more likely to have the appropriate facilities, whereas hotels on the mountainous north coast are less so. The Spanish National Tourist Office (see page 125) provides a useful fact sheet and a list of accessible accommodation.

TRAVELLING TO MALLORCA AND MENORCA

By Air *(See also* AIRPORTS *on page 104)*

Scheduled flights. Palma de Mallorca's airport is linked by daily non-stop flights to London and Frankfurt, with frequent flights to many other European cities. For intercontinental air travellers, the usual gateways to Spain are the Madrid and Barcelona airports.

Charter Flights and Package Tours. From the **U.K.** and **Eire**, an enormous choice is available. Extraordinary bargains may be on offer if you can travel at short notice, both for "flight only" tickets and for packages that include accommodation. For travellers from **North America** most charter flights operate to Madrid or the Costa del Sol, and may be combined with Mallorca in a special package.

By Road and Sea [See also CAR HIRE on page 106]

Car ferries operate daily all the year round from Barcelona and Valencia to Mallorca (an 8-hour, overnight trip); extra boats are put on in the high season, as well as direct links with Menorca, and connections with Algiers.

By Rail

Good, but crowded, trains link Spain with the rest of Europe. Seat and sleeper reservations are usually compulsory on the trains. From Barcelona, you can continue to Mallorca or Menorca by sea or by air.

Both *Inter-Rail* and *Rail Europ Senior* cards are valid in Spain, as is the *Eurailpass* for non-European residents (buy before arriving in Europe). For full information, contact the Spanish national railways: RENFE, General Agency for Europe, 1-3 av. Marceau, 75115 Paris.

WATER

Tap water in the Balearics is safe to drink; however, it can taste very flat and strange. Most local people drink bottled water, *agua con gas* (carbonated) or *sin gas* (still). It is good, clean, and inexpensive.

Mallorca and Menorca

WEIGHTS and MEASURES
For fluid and distance measures, see page 113. Spain is metric.

Weight

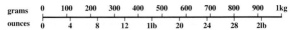

Temperature

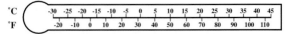

Length

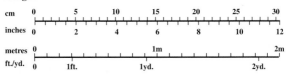

YOUTH HOSTELS *(albergue de juventud)*

These may be fully booked in summer, so you should reserve ahead:

Alberg Juvenil d'Alcúdia, La Victoria, Alcúdia, tel./fax 54 53 95. Overlooks Bay of Pollença; access by bus to Alcúdia, then taxi or 8-km (5-mile) country walk; 120 beds in 3-, 6- and 10-bedded rooms, each with shower and WC; facilities include dining hall, kitchen, terrace, TV lounge, and sports area. Closed November to March.

Alberg Platja de Palma, c/ Costa Brava 17, Ca'n Pastilla, tel./fax 26 08 92. Close to Palma and the seafront area; 65 beds in 2-, 3-, and 6-bedded rooms, each with shower and WC; other facilities include dining hall, TV lounge, terraces, and meeting hall. Open all year.

Youth Camping, Biniparratx, near Binidala, 9 km (5½ miles) from Mahón, tel. 72 02 01. 150 beds in large dormitories; dining rooms, kitchen, showers and toilets, sports field, and swimming pool.

Recommended Hotels

There is a vast number of hotels of all categories on the islands, although most are contracted to various European tour operators, thus making it virtually impossible, particularly in high season, for independent travellers to find somewhere to stay. However, we have listed below a selection of establishments that are able to provide private accommodation, grouped by location. The star rating in brackets after each entry refers to the official government grading system (see Accommodation on page 104). You are advised to book hotels well in advance, particularly if planning to visit between June and August or during a fiesta period. As a basic guide to room prices, we have used the following symbols (for a double room with bath/shower in high season):

✪	below 7,000 ptas.
✪✪	7,000-14,000 ptas.
✪✪✪	15,000-20,000 ptas.
✪✪✪✪	above 20,000 ptas.

PALMA

Hotel Almudaina (3 stars) ✪✪-✪✪✪ *Avinguda Jaime III 9, D.P. 07012; tel. 72 73 40; fax 72 25 99.* An extremely comfortable hotel in the very heart of Palma. Open all year. 80 rooms.

Hotel Meliá Confort Bellver (Sol Group) (4 stars) ✪✪✪ *Paseo Ingeniero Gabriel Roca 11, D.P. 07014; tel. 73 51 42; fax 73 14 51.* A large, modern, well-appointed hotel with restaurant and swimming pool situated in the centre of the seafront in Palma. The hotel also has facilities for disabled guests. Open all year. 389 rooms.

Hotel Son Vida (Sheraton) (5 stars) ✪✪✪✪ ++ *Urb. Son Vida 13, D.P. 07015; tel. 79 00 00; fax 79 00 17.* A luxurious hotel in every way, situated 8 km (5 miles) outside Palma in an elevated position with picturesque views over the Bay of Palma. Beautifully appointed with every facility. Golf course nearby. Open all year. 169 rooms.

WEST OF PALMA

Hotel Bon Sol (4 stars) ✪✪✪ *Paseo de Illetas 30, Illetes, D.P. 07015; tel. 40 21 11; fax 40 25 59.* An attractive family-run hotel situated on multiple levels with its own secluded beach and many other facilities including a restaurant, sun terraces, and a swimming pool. Open all year. 92 rooms.

Hotel Brismar (2 stars) ✪-✪✪ *Almirante Riera Alemany 6, Port d'Andraitx, D.P. 07157; tel. 67 16 00; fax 67 11 83.* This well-known seafront hotel located in the centre of the port area has undergone recent refurbishment and offers a restaurant and facilities for disabled guests. Conveniently situated near bus route. Closed December and January. 56 rooms.

Hotel Mar y Vent (3 stars) ✪✪ *Mayor 49, Banyalbufar, D.P. 07191; tel. 61 80 00; fax 61 82 01.* Charming family-owned and managed hotel with restaurant, terrace, and swimming pool. The views are magnificent. Closed December and January. 23 rooms.

Hotel Pûnta Negro (4 stars) ✪✪✪ *Crta. de Andraitx 12 km, Portais Nous; tel. 68 07 62; fax 68 39 19.* An extremely comfortable hotel built on several levels on its own peninsula, within easy access of secluded coves. Every facility is provided for the comfort of guests, including a swimming pool and a restaurant. Open all year. 61 rooms.

NORTHWEST COAST

El Guia (1 star) ✪ *Castañer 2, D.P. 07100, Sóller; tel. 63 02 27.* This pleasant, down-to-earth hotel is conveniently situated near to the station and offers excellent value for money. Good restaurant. Closed November to April. 20 rooms.

Hostal C'Am Mário (1 star) ✪ *c/ Vetam 8, D.P. 07170, Valldemossa; tel. 61 21 22.* This simple, pleasant hostal is conveniently situated in the centre of Valldemossa and has its own restaurant serving good local food. Closed 18 December to 12 January. 8 rooms.

Hostal Es Port (3 stars) ✪✪-✪✪✪ *Antonio Montis s/n, Port de Sóller; tel. 63 16 50; fax 63 16 62.* A very attractive hotel, one of the first in the area, with garden, sun terraces, and a picturesque view over the port. Comfortable rooms and facilities for disabled guests. Situated close to the bus route and the train/tram service from Palma. Closed December. 156 rooms.

Hotel Costa D'Or (1 star) ✪✪ *Lluch Alcari s/n, Lluch Alcari, D.P. 07179; tel. 63 90 25; fax 63 93 47.* A pleasant and comfortable hotel in an outstanding clifftop setting overlooking the sea and mountains. The hotel offers a full range of facilities, including restaurant, terraces, swimming pool, and tennis court, and is situated close to the bus route. Closed November to May. 42 rooms.

Hotel Vistamar (3 stars) ✪✪✪-✪✪✪✪ *Crta. de Andraitx 2 km, Valldemossa; tel. 61 23 00; fax 61 25 83.* A beautiful manor house hotel with excellent facilities, including a swimming pool and a superb restaurant. Closed mid-November to mid-February. 18 rooms.

Mallorca and Menorca

La Residencia (4 stars) ✪✪✪✪ ++ *Son Moragues, D.P. 07179, Deià; tel. 63 90 11; fax 63 93 70.* This elegant hotel is beautifully located in two manor houses and caters for an international clientele. The excellent facilities offered by the hotel include a highly recommended restaurant. Open all year. 271 rooms.

NORTHEAST COAST

Hotel Formentor (5 stars) ✪✪✪✪ ++ *Playa de Formentor s/n, Formentor; tel. 89 91 00; fax 86 51 55.* Beautifully appointed hotel offering both first-class facilities and a unique location. Everything is provided for the comfort of the guests, including terraces, three swimming pools, gardens, and beach area. Choice of three restaurants. Closed December and January. 127 rooms.

Hotel Niu (1 star) ✪ *Cala Barcas, Cala Sant Vicenç; tel. 53 01 00; fax 53 12 20.* A pleasant and efficient, owner-managed hotel overlooking the beach. Simple facilities provided include terraces, bar, and restaurant. Closed November to April. 24 rooms.

Illa D'Or (4 stars) ✪✪✪ *Colon 265, D.P. 07470, Port de Pollença; tel. 86 51 00; fax 86 42 13.* At the end of the Pine Walk, this well-established hotel is attractively situated at the water's edge and offers a waterside terrace and restaurant as well as tennis facilities. Disabled travellers welcome. Closed December and January. 119 rooms.

EAST/SOUTH COAST

Hostal Colonial (1 star) ✪ *Gabriel Roca 9, D.P. 07638, Colònia de Sant Jordi; tel. 65 61 82.* Small, family-run hostal in the centre of the port area. Basic but adequate accommodation presents good value for money. Restaurant. Closed November to February. 18 rooms.

Hostal Playa Mondragó (1 star) ✪ *Playa Mondragó s/n, Cala Mondragó; tel. 65 77 52; fax 65 77 52.* A modest hostal, next to the beach in a beautiful wooded setting. Facilities include swimming pool, restaurant, and beach bar. Closed November to April. 41 rooms.

Hotel Aguait (4 stars) ✪✪✪ *Avinguda de los Pinos 61, Ratigada; tel. 56 34 08; fax 56 51 06.* Quiet, wooded situation for this pleasant, comfortable hotel with swimming pool, terrace, gardens, and restaurant. Closed November to February. 188 rooms.

Hotel Cala d'Or (4 stars) ✪✪✪-✪✪✪✪ *Avinguda Belígica s/n, D.P. 07660, Cala d'Or; tel. 65 72 49; fax 65 93 51.* Attractively situated amidst pine woods just a short walk from the centre of Cala d'Or, this is an elegant hotel with an established reputation. It has recently been completely refurbished and rooms are comfortable and well appointed. Excellent facilities include swimming pool, terraces, restaurant, and beach bar. Closed November to March. 71 rooms.

Hotel Cala Marsa (3 stars) ✪✪✪ *Paseo Cala Marsal, Porto Colom; tel. 82 52 25; fax 82 52 50.* A large, comfortable beach hotel with swimming pool, tennis, garden, and terraces. There's also a restaurant and snack bar. Ideal for families and suitable for disabled guests. Closed November to May. 331 rooms.

Hotel Ses Rotges (3 stars) ✪✪ *Rafael Blanes 21, D.P. 0790, Cala Ratjada; tel. 56 31 08.* Small, very attractive and well-appointed hotel in quiet residential area close to the seafront. Michelin star restaurant. Unsuitable for children. Closed November to March. 24 rooms.

Hotel Tres Playas (4 stars) ✪✪✪ *Cala Esmeralda, D.P. 07638, Colònia de Sant Jordi; tel. 65 51 51; fax 65 56 44.* A modern and extremely well-appointed hotel set in its own garden overlooking the sea towards Es Trenc beach. There are rocks below the hotel, but a short path leads to the beach. Facilities include restaurant, swimming pool, and tennis court. Closed November to April. 118 rooms.

INLAND

Es Reco de Randa (3 stars) ✪✪-✪✪✪ *Fuente 13, Randa-Algaida, D.P. 07629; tel. 66 09 97, fax 66 25 58.* A delightful and comfortable Mallorcan manor house hotel in a village near Palma. Facilities include swimming pool and sun terrace as well as an exceptional restaurant. Open all year. 14 rooms.

Hostal Muntanya (2 stars) ✪ *Ctra. Oriente, Km 10; Orient; tel. 61 53 73.* A simple rustic *hostal* in a quiet mountain village. Excellent value accommodation. Facilities include a restaurant and terrace for outdoor dining in fine weather. Open all year. 13 rooms.

SOMETHING DIFFERENT

Ermita del Puig de María ✪ *Pollença; tel. 53 02 35.* Simple accommodation in an outstanding location. No road access, and visitors should be prepared for some stiff hiking. The custodians will provide breakfast, lunch, or dinner if required. Open all year. Very often full at weekends.

Monasteri Cura de Algada Randa ✪ *tel. 66 09 94 to reserve a room.* Basic and very economical accommodation in a tranquil location within easy access by road or on foot from Randa. Restaurant. Always fully booked in July and August.

Monasteri de Lluc ✪ *Escorca; tel. 51 70 25 to reserve a room.* Simple but comfortable accommodation in an area superb for walking. The monastery is accessible by road. Restaurant. Open all year. Always fully booked in July and August.

MENORCA

Hostal Sheila (2 stars) ✪ *Santa Cecilia 41, Mahón; tel. 36 48 55.* A family *hostal* in the heart of Mahón. Good value for money. Open all year. 12 rooms.

Hotel Capri (3 stars) ✪✪✪ *San Esteban 8, D.P. 07760, Mahón; tel. 36 14 00; fax 35 08 53.* A very comfortable and well-appointed hotel in the centre of Mahón with attractive bedrooms and spacious terraces. Restaurant. Open all year. 75 rooms.

Hotel Patricia (3 stars) ✪✪ *Paseo San Nicolás 90, D.P. 07760, Ciutadella de Menorca; tel. 38 55 11; fax 48 11 20.* A modern, well-appointed hotel in a quiet position overlooking the port of Ciutadella. Every comfort is provided for the benefit of the hotel guests. Open all year. 44 rooms.

Pension Xuroy (2 stars) ✪ *Cala Alcaufar s/n, Playa Punta Prima, Sant Lluis; tel. and fax 15 18 20.* This well-run *pension* is set in an appealingly quiet location on the edge of the beach beneath pine trees. Closed November to April. 46 rooms.

Port Mahón (4 stars) ✪✪✪✪ *Avinguda Fort de l'Eau 13, D.P. 07701, Mahón; tel. 36 26 00; fax 35 10 50.* An attractive Georgian-style mansion hotel, overlooking the harbour, and away from the centre of Mahón. Full range of facilities including swimming pool, terrace, bar, restaurant, and gardens. Open all year. 82 rooms.

Recommended Restaurants

The establishments detailed below offer a cross-section of what is available, and should convince you that not everything on the islands comes with chips (French fries). All of the restaurants listed are frequented by Spanish and Mallorcan diners, which is a sign of good, fresh local produce, ample helpings, and a fair price.

Those on a budget should ask for the *menú del día* — the daily menu — which is available at most restaurants, particularly at lunchtime. This set-price menu is about one-third of the cost of the full menu, and you will be given three generous courses. If you want to see the full menu, you should ask for *la carta* or *la lista de platos*.

Some restaurants demand a certain formality of dress, and frown on men wearing shorts and tee-shirts. For evening dining, especially, smarter clothing — including a shirt and tie — would be expected.

As a basic guide, the symbols below indicate what you should expect to pay for a three-course meal for two, excluding wine, tax, and tip. Remember that drinks will add considerably to the final bill.

✪	below 5,000 ptas.
✪✪	5,000-8,000 ptas.
✪✪✪	over 8,000 ptas.

PALMA

Asador Tierra Aranda ✪✪ *Concepció 4; tel. 71 42 56.* Succulent Castilian specialities include suckling pig, lamb, and kid roasted in traditional woodfired ovens. The ideal place for meat-eaters with healthy appetites.

Caballito del Mar ✪✪ *Paseo de Sagrera 5; tel. 72 10 74.* The place to go for fresh fish and shellfish cooked to suit your own particular requirements. There's a delightful outside terrace used for *al fresco* dining.

Celler Sa Premsa ✪ *Plaza Obispo Berenguer de Palou 8; tel. 72 35 29.* This Mallorcan dining hall is a real Palma institution. Come here at lunchtime to enjoy what the locals consider everyday fare — you'll be surprised by the wide selection. The ambience is unbeatable and it's well worth waiting for a free table. Closed Saturday and Sunday.

Koldo Royo ✪✪ *Paseo Marítimo 3; tel. 45 70 21.* Small, elegant restaurant with one Michelin star, specialising in new Basque cuisine. The food is excellent — imaginative and unusual. Dishes include quail stuffed with rose petals and goose liver. Views of the sea. Closed Saturday lunch and Sunday.

La Lubina ✪ *Muelle Viejo; tel. 72 33 50.* A simple building on the old quay of Palma overlooking the water. The daily choice of fresh fish in the display cabinet at the entrance is prepared to suit your taste.

El Pilón ✪✪-✪✪✪ *Calle San Cayetano; tel. 72 60 34.* Tucked away in a small alleyway off the Borne, this bustling restaurant is justly popular on account of its good fish and seafood dishes and its excellent *tapas*, which can be eaten before — or even instead of — lunch. The pleasant bar makes a good place to pass the time while waiting for a free table. Closed on Sunday.

Porto Pí ✪✪✪ *Avda. Joan Miró, 174; tel. 40 00 87.* Hidden away in the wrong end of town, by the port below Bellver Castle, this old Mallorcan house twinkles with a Michelin star. International dishes are prepared using fresh local ingredients and plenty of imaginative flair. An unforgettable gastronomic experience. Closed Saturday lunchtime and Sunday.

Rififi ✪✪-✪✪✪ *Avda. Joan Miró, 182; tel. 40 20 35.* A very popular seafood restaurant with a wonderful selection of dishes, from mussels to giant crayfish, all prepared to your choosing. Closed Tuesday and throughout January.

Arrocería "Sa Cranca" ✪✪✪ *Paseo Maritimo 13; tel. 73 74 47.* Elegant and expensive, this restaurant specializes in fine international cuisine and is very popular with wealthy Mallorcans. Specialities include imaginatively prepared fish dishes — the whole fish baked in rock salt is highly recommended. Closed Sunday.

WEST OF PALMA

Barlovento ✪ *Camí Vell des Far, Port d'Andraitx; tel. 67 10 49.* Built out over the sea, this is a very popular venue for locals and tourists alike — even in the winter hopeful customers wait for a free table. The restaurant's specialities are based on the daily catch of fresh seafood.

Ca'n Pedro ✪ *Archiduque Luis Salvador 6 s/n, Valldemossa; tel. 61 21 70.* Typical food of the kind Mallorcans adore — huge portions, well prepared, and excellent value for money. Closed Sunday evening and Monday.

El Patio ✪✪✪ *Ctra. Andraitx-Port d'Andraitx ; tel. 67 20 13.* A splendid restaurant recommended for its elegant atmosphere and exquisite food. The attractive terrace makes a perfect location for summer evening dining. The five-course set-price menu offers excellent value. Closed Tuesday.

Son Tomás ✪ *Baronía 17, Banyalbufar; tel. 61 81 49 .* A small bar and restaurant with a terrace and lovely views. Fresh fish comes from the boats in the cove; the *paella* and the *arroz negro* (black rice) are sumptuous. Closed Tuesdays and November to February.

Tristán ✪✪ *Puerto Punta Portals, Portals Nous; tel. 67 55 47.* Smart restaurant with two Michelin stars in this glamorous marina, with elegant outdoor dining and good views. Serves imaginative and attractive haute-cuisine dishes. Closed Mondays, and for much of January and February.

NORTH COAST

Ca'n Quet ✪✪-✪✪✪ *Crta. Deià, Deià; tel. 63 91 96.*
Renowned restaurant which specializes in international cuisine
with a unique local flavour. Very popular with Mallorcans, who
flock all the way from Palma for such delicacies as giant prawns
wrapped in puff pastry. Closed Monday.

El Guía ✪ *Castañer 3, Sóller; tel. 63 02 27.* Small, well-run
family restaurant which specializes in Mallorcan home cooking,
for which the perfect accompaniment is wine from Binissalem.
Closed Monday.

El Olivo ✪✪✪ *Son Canals, Deià; tel. 63 90 11.* For that really
special occasion, there's no better place than El Olivo, one of the
best restaurants on the island. The house speciality is
Mediterranean nouvelle cuisine, which is as delightful to the eye
as it is to the palate. There is a distinguished clientele, which
includes a number of Spanish and international celebrities.
Closed January and February.

Escorca Restaurant ✪ *Crta. Sóller-Lluc s/n; tel. 61 70 96.* A
mountain restaurant with fine views, specializing in traditional
country fare cooked over a wood stove. In autumn and winter
the excellent game dishes are particularly worth trying. Very
popular with Mallorcan families who love the Sunday lunch.
Closed in the evening and all day Wednesday.

Es Guix ✪ *Urbanizacion Es Guix Afueras Escorca s/n, Lluc;
tel. 51 70 92.* A cool, green haven in the heat of the summer,
this restaurant is equally inviting on cold winter days, when a
log fire keeps customers warm. Enjoy good Mallorcan home
cooking on the beautiful terrace, or, if you're feeling energetic,
have a dip — a surprising attraction is the restaurant's own private swimming pool. Always crowded at weekends year round.
Closed Tuesday.

Es Vergeret ✪ *Cala Tuent, Escorca; tel. 51 71 05.* Good home
cooking and excellent local wine await the intrepid visitor who

ventures up the vertiginous access road to this pleasantly uncrowded restaurant. The panoramic location, with a terrace overhanging the Cala, enhances the experience. Closed from mid-November to March.

Sa Teulera ✪-✪✪ *Crtr. Puig-Major s/n, Sóller; tel. 63 11 11.* Traditional Mallorcan roasts over a wood fire — inside or out — are the speciality, including suckling pig and rabbit. Closed Wednesday.

NORTHEAST COAST

Barlovento ✪ *Arqu. Gabriel Roca, Port de Alcúdia; tel. 54 50 48.* Excellent location near the spot where the boats come ashore, so the fish is guaranteed fresh. Highly recommended are the *arroz marinera* and *paella de mariscos*. Closed Tuesdays.

Clivia ✪✪ *Avinguda Pollentia, Pollença; tel. 53 36 75.* This elegant and tranquil restaurant is the perfect setting in which to enjoy chef Domingo's original creations. Mallorcan cuisine is given a Basque flavour especially appreciated by local Spaniards. Here you'll taste perhaps the finest mussels on the island. Closed Tuesday lunch.

La Forteleza ✪ *Crta. Formentor s/n, Port de Pollença; tel. 86 44 73.* This is where the Mallorcans go to eat, especially at weekends. An extremely well-run family restaurant, with the emphasis on home cooking and a good variety of local dishes. Renowned in particular for its *tapas* and for the best *pa amb oli con jamon serrano* to be found in Mallorca. Closed Wednesdays, and end December to March.

La Terraza ✪✪ *Plceta. Pompeu Fabra 7; tel. 54 56 11.* An attractive restaurant with a terrace overlooking the Bay of Alcúdia and the mountains. Serves well-prepared international cuisine. Closed November to Easter.

Restaurant Stay ✪✪✪ *Muelle Nuevo s/n, Port de Pollença; tel. 86 40 13.* In this smart restaurant, the choice has to be fish, but there are also imaginative meat dishes. Fresh vegetables cooked to perfection as well as an interesting choice of desserts. Highly recommended. Closed Monday, and January to February.

EAST COAST

Ca'n Martina ✪-✪✪ *Passeig des Port 56, Porto Petro; tel. 65 75 17 .* This restaurant with terrace is in a picturesque waterside setting just at the entrance to Porto Petro. Serves good seafood; the *paella de mariscos* is particularly recommended.

Los Patos ✪✪ *Ctra. Sa Pobla-Alcudia (La Albufera), km 8.9; tel. 54 69 71 .* A family-run restaurant which is extremely popular with the locals. Good Mallorcan cuisine and a friendly, lively atmosphere. A good place to take children, who are always positively welcomed here. Closed Tuesday.

Ses Rotjes ✪✪-✪✪✪ *Rafael Blanes 21, Alcedo, Cala Ratjada; tel. 56 31 08.* This French-owned *hostal* and restaurant with its Michelin star is a delightful find. A regular local clientele testifies to the consistently high standard of cuisine; reservations are advised. Closed Wednesday lunch.

INLAND

Ca'l Dimoni ✪-✪✪ *Crta., km 21, Manacor; tel. 66 56 78.* This vast barn-sized restaurant is nearly always full, noisy and typically Mallorcan. Cured sausages and hams hang down from the rafters, and the cooking is done on a large fire in the middle of the room. If you don't get here early, you'll have to be prepared to wait for a table. Closed Tuesday.

Can Romis ✪ *Plaza San Morey 14, Sencelles; tel. 87 20 88.* A simple inland Mallorcan restaurant, offering good home cooking in ample portions. Justifiably popular, particularly with the locals, not least because of the potent, locally produced house wine. Closed Monday and Tuesday evening, and mid-July to mid-August.

Mallorca and Menorca

Celler C'an Amer ✪✪ *Miguel Duran 35, C/pau 39 Inca; tel. 50 12 61.* This attractive *celler* is renowned for excellent local cooking which makes imaginative use of seasonal ingredients. Closed Sunday and Monday.

Celler Sa Travessa ✪-✪✪ *Francisco Navarro 4, C/Capau 16 Inca; tel. 50 00 49.* Another very attractive *celler* restaurant which serves good local cuisine. The place is very popular with the Mallorcans. Closed on Friday.

Es Cuatre Vents Z ✪✪✪ *Crta. Palma-Manacor, km 21.7, Manacor, Algaida; tel. 66 51 73.* Extremely popular with the locals — a little more sophisticated than Ca'l Dimoni and somewhat less noisy. The choice of dishes here is immense. Reservations are essential for Sunday lunchtime. Closed Thursday.

Es Reco de Randa ✪✪-✪✪✪ *Font 13, Randa; tel. 66 04 97.* This delightful restaurant set in a country hotel is worth driving across the island for. The choice and quality of food are exceptional. International cuisine is served in addition to many Mallorcan specialities. A reservation is highly advisable.

Orient Restaurant ✪-✪✪ *Orient s/n; tel. 61 51 53.* Very popular Mallorcan cuisine. The house specialities are suckling pig, lamb, and *frit Mallorquí*. The restaurant can become very busy, so for lunch make sure you arrive before 1pm, or, better still, phone and reserve a table in advance. Closed Monday.

Ses Porxeres ✪✪-✪✪✪ *Crta. Palma-Soller, km 17, Bunyola; tel. 61 37 62.* One of the best restaurants on the island, serving exceptional Mallorcan and Catalan cuisines. Specialities here include enormous starters (appetizers), game, fish stews, and lamb cutlets grilled on hot rocks at your table, all rounded off with *crema catalan*. Reservations essential for Sunday lunch. Closed on Sunday evening, Monday, and throughout August.

MENORCA

Alba ✪ *Moll de Llevant 36, Mahón; tel. 35 06 06.* Attractive pavement terrace ideal for summertime dining. Specialities include carefully prepared fish dishes, and the menu is changed daily. Excellent value. Closed November to April.

Casa Manolo ✪-✪✪ *Marina 117, Port de Ciutadella; tel. 38 00 03.* Specializes in a wide choice of freshly caught fish, prepared to a very high standard, to suit your tastes. Very popular.

Ca's Quinto ✪ *Plaza de Alfonso III 4, Ciutadella; tel. 38 10 02.* Simple bar/restaurant specializing in fish and shellfish at reasonable prices.

Es Moli des Raco ✪-✪✪ *Vicario Fuxa 53, Es Mercadal; tel. 37 53 92.* Attractive country-style restaurant set in an old mill with a pleasant terrace for summer dining. Always a good menu of the day. Specialities include stuffed vegetables and traditional Menorcan dishes. It is essential to make reservations for evening dining during the high season.

Es Pla ✪-✪✪ *Pasaje Es Pla, Fornells; tel. 37 66 55.* One of many typical fish restaurants; this one is very popular with the locals. The baked fish and *caldereta de langosta* are highly recommended.

Gregal ✪-✪✪ *Martires de Atlante 43, Mahón; tel. 36 66 06.* Situated in the port with fine views. Popular lunchtime venue with local businesspeople, which becomes a meeting place for the smart set in the evenings. Specialities are fish and shellfish. Open all year round.

Mesón El Gallo ✪✪ *Crta. Cala Galdana, 1.5 km, Ferrerías; tel. 37 30 39.* A family-run restaurant in an old farmhouse, specializing in Menorcan home cooking using local meat. The *paella del gallo* should not be missed. Regular clientele. Closed Monday.

ABOUT BERLITZ

In 1878 Professor Maximilian Berlitz had a revolutionary idea about making language learning accessible and enjoyable. One hundred and twenty years later these same principles are still successfully at work.

For language instruction, translation and interpretation services, cross-cultural training, study-abroad programs, and an array of publishing products and additional services, visit any one of our more than 350 Berlitz Centers in over 40 countries.

Please consult your local telephone directory for the Berlitz Center nearest you or visit our web site at http://www.berlitz.com.

Helping the World Communicate